# WHISK(E)Y
## DISTILLED

# WHIS

## HEATHER GREENE

# K(E)Y
## DISTILLED

### A POPULIST GUIDE TO
### THE WATER OF LIFE

*Heather Greene*
*Slainté!*
♡ XO

VIKING STUDIO

VIKING STUDIO
Published by the Penguin Group
Penguin Group (USA) LLC
375 Hudson Street
New York, New York 10014

USA | CANADA | UK | IRELAND | AUSTRALIA | NEW ZEALAND | INDIA | SOUTH AFRICA | CHINA

penguin.com

A Penguin Random House Company

First published by Viking Studio, a member of Penguin Group (USA) LLC, 2014

Copyright © 2014 by Heather Greene

Photographs © Steve Giralt

Drawings by John Burgoyne

LIBRARY OF CONGRESS CATALOGING-IN-PUBLICATION DATA

Greene, Heather.
Whiskey distilled : a populist guide to the water of life / Heather Greene.
pages cm
Includes index.
ISBN 978-0-670-01680-8
1. Whiskey. I. Title.
TP605.G76 2014
663'.52—dc23
2014022310

Printed in the United States of America

1 3 5 7 9 10 8 6 4 2

Designed by Renato Stanisic

TO MS. KATHLEEN MARY ORR (AKA MOM)

*Who's always up for travel, shenanigans,*
*and drinking whiskey with me*

# CONTENTS

# Introduction:
# What's a Spirits Sommelier?

THIS IS A BOOK about whiskey, so I will begin it by describing my own first taste one summer between eighth and ninth grades. It happened on a Saturday afternoon behind Kenny Bash's house. Kenny was the neighborhood troublemaker. As I sat on the hard plastic board of his rusted-out, squeaky swing set, dragging my bare feet back and forth on a patch of dirt, he handed me a plastic liter container of bright orange soda and commanded, "Take a sip." After a quick swig, I gagged, and his cruel bray of adolescent laughter followed. "Take more," he said. "It's Jack." This was dangerous territory and I knew it.

In a panic, I hurried back home, terrified that my parents would find out about the Jack. I shoved a fistful of grass into my mouth—I'd heard that grass hides the smell of alcohol. When my parents didn't notice, I thanked my lucky stars and promised myself that I'd never drink whiskey again.

I've spent the past ten years breaking that promise.

Today I am the Director of Whiskey Education at The Flatiron Room Whiskey School in Manhattan and I teach whiskey classes there every week. I'm also the restaurant's sommelier, which is a word that comes from nineteenth-century French and essentially means butler. I didn't sit whiskey tests to become one (there aren't any) nor do I mean to turn anyone off with a word that can sound pretentious. Truth is, what I do is very butler-like: I roam the floor, serve guests, and pluck a few personal details out of them to help them find the whiskey they will love. "What wine or cocktail do you normally drink?" I might ask, or, "What do you like to eat?" Then I'll hunt down the perfect whiskey—out of the thousand or so The Flatiron Room stocks—to suit their palate. On days I'm not at The Flatiron Room, I write about whiskey for a couple of magazines. And when I'm not doing that, I'm often out on the town with a friend or my husband, checking out a new cocktail bar or restaurant that serves my favorite spirit. I guess you could say I've essentially built a career on drinking Jack.

In a move my colleagues and a few friends found odd, in 2012 I left my "sweet-ass" job as a "whiskey ambassador" to join The Flatiron Room and write. As an ambassador to Glenfiddich, "world's number one selling single malt Scotch," I enjoyed dazzling perks like international travel and a corporate card that allowed me to buy a nice steak dinner for dozens at high-end strip joints and country clubs, if you're into that sort of thing. I can rattle off some of the best places in the United States to find hedonistic entertainment, and I've played golf (badly) on famous courses like those at Turnberry in Scotland. I even climbed Kilimanjaro in Tanzania for charity during a blizzard wearing Glenfiddich-branded gear, and slept in it too, perched on the side of a cliff in a quivering tent. At each dinner, corporate function, golf tournament, charity gala, magazine interview, TV spot, fashion show, private yacht trip, private plane trip, car show, and even rodeo, my role was the same: to make my audience fall in love with whiskey. Oh, and to use Glenfiddich while doing it.

Someone asked every other night whether I "really liked Glenfiddich" or if there was some other whiskey I secretly drank in private. While I never admitted that I had secret lovers, I'd be true in my answer: I chose to work as an ambassador for Glenfiddich because I liked it in the first place, not the other way around. It's also a brand that aficionados love for its collectibility and taste—I stood next to a bidder at the base of the Statue of Liberty during a Glenfiddich charity auction and watched in awe as he won the bottle for close to a hundred thousand dollars. It was a good gig.

But relationships evolve. I started to feel a nagging love for bourbon, rye, Japanese whiskies, Irish whiskeys, and a bevy of other exciting spirits, and soon I needed to spend more time with them, too. So Glenfiddich and I split. Whiskey monogamy just isn't my thing. By the end of this book, it won't be yours, either.

The most important thing I've learned by hosting events—whether they're for a hundred corporate executives on behalf of a big whiskey company or for two guests at The Flatiron Room—is how to talk about it. And, while speaking to thousands (yes, that's right, *thousands*) of whiskey drinkers, my goal is to demystify whiskey and answer questions like: How do you taste whiskey? What are you supposed to smell? Do you swirl whiskey like wine? Can you put ice in a whiskey? Water? What does "small batch" mean? Why is Johnnie Walker Blue so expensive? What is moonshine? Why does this bottle say non–chill filtered? How do you store it? Can you make money by investing in it? Can women drink it?

Today, American whiskey sales alone top $1 billion, up from $376 million about a decade ago. Its popularity is growing faster than the good information available on the topic. And some of the advice out there is just plain off the mark. I've read blogs written by brutish whiskey fans that say certain (critically acclaimed) brands aren't even good enough to use as a toilet cleaner, and that to drink them means you have no taste. But taste is subjective. I've heard brand ambassadors explain that whiskey won't make you drunk, but tequila will. Nonsense. I read nosing notes on Web sites and in books that go on for as many pages as *Moby Dick*. But the truth is, most experts can realistically identify five distinct aromas. I listened to a tourist guide for a famous American whiskey distillery explain to thirty of us that all Scotch tastes like smoke. Not true. My role here, then, is to sift through all the junky information out *there*, and give you a real primer of whiskeys, so that you'll be able to identify bunk like a champ and become an expert yourself. You'll taste along the way and have fun, too.

## AND THE NUMBER ONE
## QUESTION IS...?

"How did someone like *you* [a chick] get into whiskey?" It's a question asked a dozen times per day and sometimes I just don't feel like explaining myself—I'd prefer to get right into nosing and tasting. But someone like *me* needs to "establish credibility," according to one CEO who attended my tasting. I resisted that advice for years, but he was right. Now I always explain my background. The result? First, guests cease fact-checking things I say with their iPhones tucked under the table, and second, I don't have to answer "Do you really drink this stuff?" after I've taught a ninety-minute class.

### How I Got into Whiskey

Before whiskey, there was music. As a professional solo musician for close to ten years, I poured my heart and soul into the creation of song, the rigor of touring, the passion of singing, and the pure joy of playing keyboard. I had recorded two albums, which received wildly wonderful reviews in New York City, and I was performing in front of rapidly growing audiences.

From the outside, my music career appeared wonderfully on track, but my bank account told a different story. After I'd had one sold-out concert in New York City, an appearance on WFUV in New York, and even a European *Rolling Stone* review in anticipation of an upcoming tour, a friend (who had also just completed a European tour with a world-famous musician) asked me for twenty bucks because "cash flow was tough." We were on the corner of Broadway and 4th Street, right next to a boarded-up Virgin Records store. I went to get money, and instead of hearing the comforting electronic patter of bills being sorted inside the ATM machine, the dreaded Funds Not Available sign flashed on the screen. We walked back to the club where we had just performed and shamelessly asked our bass-player friend to get us both—two "professional" musicians—home in his truck. The advent of new technology and iTunes had officially tossed the music world upside down, and none of us were making money anymore. What should have started looking like a lucrative (finally!) career became a barrage of confusion, record-label fights, and overall heartbreak for just about every musician I knew, including myself.

Around this same time, my husband was accepted to graduate school in Edinburgh, Scotland. We packed our stuff and left Manhattan during the fall of 2005. I very quickly went from a "struggling musician with promise" to a struggling musician, period. The high of an Italian performance in Rome was followed by the lows of phone calls I made begging the label to pay me what they owed. My life became an emotional roller coaster, and I was terribly homesick for the fast-paced New York life we'd left, with my community of musicians, weekly gigs, and the easy access to recording studios. During one of my lavish pity parties, my husband turned to me and said that I *really* needed to do something. So I went out drinking.

I was hired on my first day out "looking for something to do" by a gentleman called Douglas McFarlane, who spoke with a chowder-thick Scottish accent and managed the Scotch Malt Whisky Society (SMWS), a private membership bar for Scotch whisky lovers. I learned about the job by reading a Help Wanted ad in a local paper and it seemed like a fun way to meet some cool people and be Scottish-y. In my experience, working in restaurants and bars immerses one quickly into a local scene and its cast of characters. That it was a whisky venue was a total bonus. I'd discovered that I liked whiskey when I was working as a waiter at the Union Square Café in Manhattan. The beverage director there had conducted a few whiskey tastings to help the staff better sell the stuff and I realized that there was more to whiskey than taking a shot or mixing it with Coke.

The SMWS lives in a corner of a Harry Potter–esque seventeenth-century green and wet stone building. Two large fireplaces flank one side of an oak-lined room. One of the employees would later show me how to wrap my fingers around panels, moldings, door frames, and windowsills to scale the periphery of the room without touching the floor, like a rock climber. That's what British schoolboys sometimes do, I learned. To the left of the front entrance of the room, there is an exquisite collection of whiskey, representing almost every distillery that has ever operated in Scotland. Bottles line shelves in neat rows and bartenders serve whisky from a small, shiny wooden bar. Members take their "dram" to one of a few long library tables and enjoy it alongside the daily paper and a tuna sandwich. When I worked there, guests at SMWS included a smattering of locals who chatted about how to salmon fish or grow brambles, and a few passing American Scotch-drinking enthusiasts on their way to play golf at places like St. Andrews.

I spent my first day at the SMWS with Doug, tasting cask-strength whisky (whisky straight out of the cask at a higher proof), playing with a miniature whisky-making model, and testing my sensory skills with a nosing kit that always sat on the bar for guests to test their sense of smell. The kit held little samples of lavender, herbs, spices, and vanilla tucked into little glass jars. Douglas's passion for whisky echoed my own for writing songs and performing; he talked about flavor and smell with the same fervor I talked about keyboard riffs. I was hooked—creativity and sensuality lived in whisky making and appreciation, too. From that point on, my life would be a balancing act between two great loves.

Within a few months of my working at SMWS, Doug invited me to sit with a bunch of whisky experts to do cask tastings and discuss whether the whiskies we tried were delicious enough to bottle and sell under the SMWS label. In a strange twist of fate, one of the regular panelists backed out for a singing gig, so I took his spot. I was very nervous. I was still a student, I felt, not yet someone worthy enough to be on a judging panel.

Tasting whiskey and writing notes about it, it turns out, is a good time. I approached the task the same way I'd sit down to write a song: without self-ridicule and with eagerness. And because I had worked in so many Manhattan restaurants with killer wine lists, I figured some of the same notes I used to describe wine to guests could also describe whiskey characteristics. I was right. Whiskey, wine, and even music share a common language or, pun intended, notes. Here are a few examples that come to mind: "vanilla" (Barry Manilow), "honeyed" (Ella Fitzgerald), "complex" (Bob Dylan), "rich" (Adele), "fresh and thin" (Taylor Swift), "bold" (Eminem), and "smoky" (Peggy Lee).

So there you have it. I honed my whiskey chops by both channeling my passion for music into it and capitalizing on a wine vocabulary amassed from years of restaurant work.

## A NOTE FOR YOU WINE LOVERS

I make comparisons between whiskey and wine throughout the book because I know many of you come to whiskey with a working knowledge of the wine world. I see this in my classes and in the type of questions I get, like "What vintage is particularly good for whiskey?" Pascaline Lepeltier, a skilled sommelier who runs what *The New York Times* called the best wine program in New York City at Rouge Tomate, has given me some additional insight about whiskey from the wine perspective. We once hosted a class together called Whiskey for the Wine Lover, and I admired her ability to help narrow whiskey choices based on wine so much that I'm including her recommendations in this book. I'm also excited about our quick-look whiskey versus wine chart. You'll find both of these charts in the appendix at the end of the book.

## WE'LL MAKE COCKTAILS, TOO

Hemant Pathak and Alex Valencia, two bartenders I work with at The Flatiron Room, will provide you with ingredients and techniques for how to make a fabulous whiskey cocktail in chapter 5. The three of us spent countless hours experimenting with different whiskeys, each with varying flavor profiles, to come up with a few fun cocktails for you to try at home. We've included both simple concoctions and ones that challenge the skillful chef. I don't know many bartenders who are skilled at making such mind-blowing whiskey drinks as these men are, but what really impresses me about both Alex and Hemant is their elegance and humility behind the bar, as well as the cultural element they bring to their cocktail making. Hemant, who was born and raised in India, will cultivate your whiskey love by combining the spirit with ingredients like cardamom and Darjeeling while Alex's playful use of smoke and fruit are a nod to mescal and the vibrant colors that surrounded him as a boy in Mexico.

But first, the fundamentals. In the next few chapters, we'll dive headfirst into the basics: whiskey appreciation, how to discover your palate, whiskey regions, and whiskey making 101. And the best part? I'll guide you through tastings in each chapter. And, I'll cultivate your whiskey love by introducing you to distillers, writers, master blenders, scientists, chefs, restaurant owners, and even whiskey-loving presidents.

So drink up! We've got a whole world of whiskey to explore.

# WHISK(E)Y
## DISTILLED

# 1

## Whiskey Fundamentals

*Appreciation 101 and Finding Your Palate*

### WHAT IS WHISKEY?

My mother flew across the Atlantic to visit me while I was living in Scotland and we took a road trip. On the third day of her stay, she announced that she absolutely needed to hear Gaelic being spoken by native speakers—somehow this mission would help her have a more "authentic" Scottish experience. She had just finished gathering clumps of Scottish dirt into plastic Baggies, which she then tied in knots, prepping them for a sneaky journey back into the U.S.A. (it's illegal to bring in peat through customs), when she asked, "What are you looking at? It's *peat*. Don't you know what peat is?" I didn't. I also didn't expect I'd be accompanying her an hour later on a pretend shopping trip to a random food market on the side of the road to catch the Gaelic-speaking species in their true habitat. I indulged her romantic vision of an authentic Scottish experience by following her as she chased down old ladies with her shopping cart. Near a shelf stacked with British teas, she whispered to me, "Oh my God, I think that lady shopping over there just said something in Gaelic. Did you hear that?" Life is full of unexpected twists and turns, and now, years later, I, too, find myself sneaking peat past U.S. Customs, then burning it during my whiskey classes to demonstrate how its earthy smell gets into some whiskeys and speaking a couple of Gaelic terms in the process.

## "Whiskey" Is a Gaelic Word

Meaning "water of life," "whiskey" started out as "usquebaugh," phonetically becoming "usky," and now, the easily pronounceable word you are familiar with if you picked up this book. Whiskey, at its core, is simply a distilled spirit made from grain, yeast, and water. But I'll bedazzle you with the cornucopia of whiskey flavors and styles that develop from those three ingredients. When a guest at The Flatiron Room tells me he or she doesn't like whiskey, I proudly point to the vast array of whiskey bottles sitting like soldiers on the shelves and say, "There's a whiskey to suit every palate!"

## Whiskey Is Worldwide

You can be sure that wherever grains grow around the world, some crafty person probably made whiskey from them. And, like wine, whiskey has a rich history that can be categorized quite simply, by region. Whiskey from a particular region often expresses character traits unique to that place, and will depend on factors such as the grain, terroir, whiskey-making methods and equipment, history, and even government laws that dictate what sort of label is allowed on a bottle and how the whiskey must be made.

> Terroir (te rwär): A term traditionally used in the wine world, "terroir" refers to environmental factors such as soil, water, climate, and topography that can influence flavor.

For example, you probably know that Champagne is a crisp and toasty sparkling white (or rosé) wine hailing from the famous Champagne region of France. A vineyard can make a similar style wine in California, but that vineyard cannot call it Champagne. Instead, they'll call it a sparkling California wine. In Spain, they make Cava, and in Italy, they make sparkling styles like Prosecco, Asti, and Lambrusco. Each region produces a slightly different style of sparkling wine under a different name and with different grapes, methods, terroir, and regulations. The whiskey world operates in much the same way. Whiskey from Scotland, for example, we call Scotch, and whiskey from America we call American whiskey. Japan, Ireland, and Canada are also big whiskey-producing countries with some incredible and historic distilleries that are now duking it out with some feisty newcomers like France, India, Sweden, and Taiwan. Instead of using different grapes as winemakers do, whiskey makers use different grains as well as different methods and operate under unique government regulations and in various terroirs.

## "WHISKEY" IS AN UMBRELLA TERM

Single malt Scotches. Blended Scotches. Bourbons. Ryes. Irish whiskeys. These are all types of whiskeys, which may seem obvious to some readers, but the most common question in every whiskey course I teach is, "Is bourbon a whiskey?" Or, "I don't like whiskey, what sort of Scotches can you recommend?" "Whiskey" is an umbrella term: All bourbons are whiskeys, but not all whiskeys are bourbons.

## Whiskey's Regional Subcategories

We can dig deeper into whiskey-making regions and discover different subcategories. In America, there's American *bourbon* whiskey and American *rye* whiskey, among others. In Scotland, there are five subtypes; among them are single malt Scotch and blended Scotch, the two most widely exported styles.

A whiskey maker must also follow local rules in order to call its bottled liquid bourbon or single malt Scotch whisky. Organizations such as the American Alcohol and Tobacco Tax and Trade Bureau (TTB) regulate whiskey language and contents. Labels can get downright confusing: non–chill filtered, cask strength, single malt Scotch from Speyside, anyone? In America, it's often what's left *unsaid* that will unlock what's inside. And Ireland? I'll fill you in on what "pot still" means to them, which is different from anything else in the whiskey-making world. You'll crack those codes and be able to predict a whiskey's taste by reading the label—regions such as Speyside and Islay will sound as familiar to you as French wine-making areas like Bordeaux and Champagne.

## "WHISKEY" VERSUS "WHISKY"

"I'm looking out there for the one person who apparently was not offended by the spelling of 'whiskey' in my column on Speyside single malts. . . ."—Eric Asimov, *The New York Times*, December 4, 2008, in response to his "whiskey versus whisky" snafu

In late 2008, *New York Times* food and wine columnist Eric Asimov wrote an article on single malt Scotch. At the time, *The New York Times* style guide encouraged the use of "whiskey" as the spelling when writing of the category. Asimov did precisely that—and the article was met with some serious rage. Comments poured in from all over the world, criticizing him for his "unforgivable use" of "whiskey" when he was speaking clearly and uniquely of Scotch "whisky." Whiskey lovers from the U.K. wrote to the *Times* to let Asimov know how disrespectful he'd been, and others hammered his story, claiming they couldn't even read the content through the blatant misspelling. Other *New York Times* readers reduced the detractors to nothing more than "Scotch snobs," which, quite frankly, I thought was ironic— whisky loving in Scotland is far from snobbery, even if in America those two words—"Scotch" and "snob"—are often drawn together like magnets. You are more likely to share drams with a local lorry driver finishing his weekly whisky transport down the A1 to Glasgow from Dufftown than with someone holding the latest literary novel or a golf club. Entire towns rely on the economics of a local distillery, with generations of families working in the bottling plants, still houses, mash rooms, and maturation warehouses. *The New York Times*'s decision to alter the spelling of Scotland's most beloved export chipped away at its national pride and place in libation history.

In the end, Asimov followed up with a blog post to explain himself and to announce that the paper would from that point on differentiate between the two spellings.

My favorite theory behind the difference between "whisky" and "whiskey" dates back to the nineteenth century when either the Irish or Americans—it isn't exactly clear—wanted to differentiate between their spirit and the spirit that the Scottish made. Some sources say it was because the Americans and Irish wanted to show the superiority of their spirits over the Scottish hooch and others say exactly the opposite. I honor whatever spelling that particular region asks for and spell it that way.

Here's an easy way to remember it: Scotland, Japan, and Canada spell whisky without an *e*. (A good way to remember this is to look at the letters in the countries' names: no *e*!)

America and Ireland spell their whiskeys with an *e*. (And both countries' names have the letter *e*.) This is how I've seen others keep track of the spelling.

Don't feel like keeping track? Daunted by exceptions like Maker's Mark from Kentucky, which spells its brand without the *e* like the Scots do? Don't worry. The bottle on the shelf will tell you exactly how they spell it—put your brain to rest. In this book I will interchange the spelling depending on the country to which I'm referring. If I'm speaking of the whiskey category as a whole, I'll use the *e* because that's the default American way.

I'm also happy to report that you (yes, you!) will master and appreciate many different whiskeys simply by nosing and tasting them without even looking at the label. Think about this: If I handed you a glass of red wine and a glass of sparkling white and then quizzed you on which one was the Champagne, you might be insulted. Of course you know the difference. My goal? By the end of this book you'll know when you are drinking an American whiskey rather than a Scotch because you'll immediately identify the unique combination of typical robust American whiskey notes that often give it away. It's an impressive party trick.

Will you become a Scotch whisky geek like me when I first started my own journey? Will you start a collection that reflects a passion for whiskeys that are made at the new, small distilleries now dotting the American landscape? You'll find out, but first let me help you learn the basics of whiskey drinking so that you can start forming your own whiskey personality. Don't worry, we'll get to drinking soon (with our first tasting).

# A PRIMER ON WHISKEY APPRECIATION

### First Things First: Say Hello to Your Nose!

Your nose is your very best friend when it comes to whiskey appreciation. If you haven't given your olfactory system much love before, just imagine how exciting it will be to discover the depths of your own nosing talents. Who knows? You might rouse a sleeping beast. That's what happened to me—I didn't know how sensitive I was to smell until I moved to Scotland and was tested on it, an experience I describe in a bit. Now my whole career depends on it. If I get the slightest cold, I become seriously worried—I even found a whiskey-loving doctor who calls me back immediately when I have any issues (and allows me to wax poetic about bourbon while he's writing my scripts). My nose love is so grand that I've traveled in midtown traffic during a blizzard to get to his office. I've witnessed that latent nosing talent and excitement blossom in students, waiters, guests, and bartenders who amaze me by picking out notes I miss. Now some of them make award-winning cocktails for magazines or collect whiskey with such confidence that they've become the whiskey "expert" in their own circles. One of my students was so inspired that he's started building a photography career with whiskey as his subject, even landing a cover story in a magazine. Soon you'll too wake up with your newfound talent and feel like you did the first time you watched sports on high-definition TV or listened to music through a killer set of speakers: Everything tunes up and pulses. You'll drive your friends a bit crazy, and you'll start to admire or even feel a wee bit jealous of your dog.

### Nose News Is Good News: No Training Necessary

You don't need any special training or knowledge to begin identifying aromas in a whiskey. Your olfactory system maps directly to the most ancient part of your brain—the limbic system, the system connected to emotion and memory—so your nose knows what to do quite naturally. At the beginning, you may get only an image of a time or place, like "Christmas" or "ocean," rather than a concrete aromatic descriptor like "cloves." So be it. Describe the image. The idea is to get comfortable with your sense of smell so you can take better advantage of it.

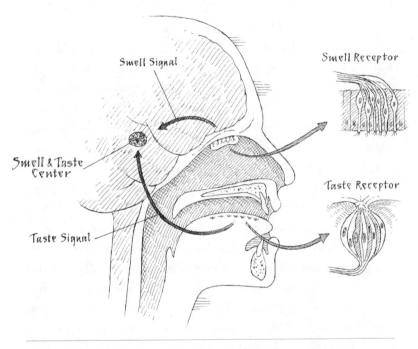

*Whiskey aromatics stimulate receptors in the roof of our nasal cavity, which send messages to our brain. Similarly, when we taste whiskey, we stimulate receptors on our tongue that also send messages to our brain. The information then converges in the temporal lobe to give us an overall flavor of our whiskey.*

The best thing to do while you are practicing with aromas is to relax and trust yourself and your instincts. Don't get frustrated if you have trouble pinpointing any kind of descriptor at first. Dr. Rachel Herz, author of *The Scent of Desire* and a world-renowned expert on the psychology of smell, says we may have trouble simultaneously nosing and speaking because the two activities interfere with each other in the brain. She calls it "language-olfactory interference," and research on the topic is newly under way. I witness this phenomenon every time I teach—I'll ask my students for a few words that come to mind after they nose a glass, only to be met with radio silence. Now I give my new students a dozen or so evocative words to think about while they taste whiskey so that they can relax and let their noses do the work. I'll give you a language to talk about whiskey later in this chapter: Use it as a crutch for a while so you don't feel lost or silly. It will help you get started as we go through our first tasting. Soon, you'll build your own framework and unique vocabulary. You just need practice, some creativity, and the confidence to know that your observations are just as valid as anyone else's.

### How I Found My Nose

When I was first learning about whiskey, I faced a big nosing challenge in a laboratory with one of the most renowned master blenders in the industry—Rachel Barrie, who now works at Morrison Bowmore Distillers. Was I nervous? You bet. Not only is she at the top of her whiskey game, she rides motorcycles and holds a PhD in chemistry to boot—the epitome of cool in my world. I also happen to suffer from test anxiety. As a young girl I had the remarkable ability to fail quizzes. But this nosing challenge was a screening test to get into one of Rachel's coveted workshops. I needed to bring my A game.

Rachel led me into a characterless laboratory inside the Glenmorangie Distillery headquarters located outside of Glasgow where she worked at the time. (The distillery, however, is located in the Highlands, a different region of Scotland.) Twenty small vials filled with cotton balls soaked in a specific identifiable scent were lined up before me like Matchbox cars ready for a race. With a couple quick breaths to relax myself, I dove in. "Write what you smell," Rachel said. Simple enough.

But when I opened each little tincture and inhaled, I immediately experienced a disconnect between the smell and the word for the smell—the exact phenomenon Dr. Herz studies. I went back to the beginning of the lineup and started over again, spending more time with each scent, until the aroma triggered something I could name. One vial's scent brought me back to a dinner my mother had prepared during one of her more experimental cooking phases when I was in middle school. The meal included spiced curried chicken pieces over rice, with little bowls of shredded coconut, raisins, bananas, and nuts for garnish and spice. I ran through the list of the dish's ingredients in my head until a word snapped into place to describe the aroma, "Ahhh . . . coconut." In the end, remembering that dinner helped me nail the scent.

I waited nervously as Rachel tallied my results, knowing I needed a score of 85 or above to get into the workshop. I played mental games with myself: If I got a "good" score, I was meant to work in the field. If not, I'd do something else—maybe take up Scottish salmon fly-fishing. This was before I realized that practice makes perfect when it comes to nosing (and before I found out that I'm the worst angler ever—I know a Scotsman with a puncture wound and a sour memory to prove that).

I did *really* well—an extraordinary feat for a serial test flunker. It was as though the whiskey gods blessed me with some confidence to start a new career. "Congratulations! You are an excellent noser," Rachel wrote to me in an e-mail. My score was a rock-solid 94.

But you don't have to fly to Scotland and sit in a laboratory under the guidance of a master blender to find your nose. The scents will trigger different memories for you, and it can be experiences—a meal you remember, a childhood event—that will help you hone your nose. You may be surprised by the associations you make. I've smelled a pillowcase filled with Halloween trick-or-treat candy. Maybe you'll smell cheap perfume. I'm all for whiskey notes describing Jean Naté and Giorgio circa 1987, if you are old enough to remember your first date wearing those scents.

## WOMEN MAY NOSE BEST

Many women can rattle off whiskey notes like a Kentucky Derby race announcer—and right out of the gate, too. Olfactory neuropsychologist Dr. Charles Wysocki says that women's superior sense of smell stems from biology, namely, that women enjoy this ability because scent is how women select mates. Studies show that body odor packs genetic information that women can detect.

You've probably heard someone say, "We didn't have the right chemistry." As it turns out, it might be absolutely correct. In a study now famously (if not unappetizingly) called the "sweaty T-shirt study" conducted in 1995 in Switzerland by Claus Wedekind, a group of men were asked to wear the same T-shirt for two days sans cologne, soap, or any other fragrance. After two days, the T-shirts were placed in boxes with small holes cut into the sides. Women were tasked to smell the airspace within those boxes through the holes, with the T-shirts still inside, and to rate them in terms of sexual attraction. Consistently, women rated T-shirts infused with a body odor from a man with different major histocompatibility complex (MHC) genes as more sexy than those T-shirts from men with similar MHC genes. It is believed that the more varied the MHC genes, the more an offspring is able to defend against illness and disease. Therefore, women tend to choose mates with MHC genes very dissimilar from their own—all based on an enhanced ability to smell them.

Not convinced? Another smell-based study conducted out of the Monell Chemical Senses Center in Philadelphia—

run by Dr. Wysocki—asked women to rate sweat odors, too. In this case, the goal of the study was to explore whether or not fragrance can mask these odors. While sweat presented on its own smelled equally strong to men and women, after "masking" with fragrance, women were still able to detect the underlying scent, while men couldn't. So much for men's cologne. Guys: No matter how much AXE you douse yourself in, we can still smell the gym.

To the men reading this, please don't despair. While the sense of smell can come more *naturally* to women, it doesn't mean that all women are better than all men. Nosing is also a highly teachable skill that with time and practice can be finely honed.

## The Big Whiskey Secret Revealed: Nose Is Everything

I'm going to spend a lot of time talking to you about our noses because the reality about whiskey appreciation is this: All whiskey pretty much *tastes* the same. By taste, I mean our ability to detect sweet, salty, bitter, sour, and umami (a Japanese word used to describe a savory or meaty taste) through the receptors on our tongues. We simply cannot appreciate or even identify different whiskeys without *using our noses*.

I make this bold claim because it's so easy to prove—just put a bunch of whiskeys in a row, plug your nose, and see for yourself. You won't notice much taste difference among them. I learned this fascinating fact at the Monell Chemical Senses Center, a scientific institute for smell and taste in Philadelphia. I'd gone there to learn the olfactory and gustatory (taste) mechanics behind my favorite whiskey and food pairings. For example, why does steak seem to complement whiskeys so well? (I'll talk more about this in chapter 6.) But before we even got to talking about food and whiskey, scientist and head of communications at

Monell, Dr. Leslie Stein, suggested we begin our session by placing blue clamps on our noses and tasting pure ethanol out of a beaker, followed by American moonshine, American bourbon whiskey, American rye whiskey, single malt Scotch whisky, and finally, a heavily peat-smoked whisky called Laphroaig. She wanted to first establish what each whiskey tasted like, without any influence from our noses.

She carefully created a rudimentary chart on a whiteboard so we could record our observations. We started with pure ethanol and moved through the rest of the list. What was shocking was that with our noses plugged, we couldn't discern the ethanol from the other whiskeys, or one whiskey from any of the other whiskeys, even though they came from various whiskey regions and carried many distinct and vibrant aromas like smoke. Dr. Stein was thrilled with our initial findings. "This is exciting," she said. "It doesn't happen like this with wine or beer!" This was new for them, too. I was floored. Everything I thought I knew about whiskey appreciation and evaluation would now require a different approach. I knew that nosing was important, but I just didn't know to what extent. The theory is that somehow whiskey's high alcohol content really messes with our taste receptors.

Since my visit to the Monell laboratory, I've done this experiment many times with colleagues and students. With their noses plugged, no one can really tell any difference between major whiskey styles. So now I torture students in classes with a twenty-minute lecture on nosing before I let them even touch a glass.

### The Science of Smell, or Your Second Chance to Ace Tenth-Grade Chemistry (This Time, with Booze)

Because nosing is so important to whiskey appreciation, let's back up for a moment and talk about what's really going on when we experience aroma. Incredibly: Scientists now know that humans can detect about a trillion different smells. Most of them will enter your nose in the form of organic molecular compounds. What are molecular compounds? You may remember from high school chemistry that molecules are formed when two or more atoms of an element (remember that periodic table of elements?) join together to form a chemical bond—they share or exchange electrons. Some molecules form with only two atoms of the same element, like oxygen ($O_2$). When two or more different elements bond together, such as hydrogen and oxygen for water ($H_2O$), we call it a compound. *All compounds are molecules, but not all molecules are compounds.* An organic molecular compound contains a combination of some or all of the following elements: hydrogen, oxygen, sulfur, nitrogen, and carbon. It's the presence of carbon that allows us to call a molecule organic.

Guess what? Molecules smell! These volatile molecules fly off of steaks, beer, ice cream, strawberries, hair gel, perfumes, flowers, bubble gum, gas pumps, and, unfortunately, foul puddles on subway platforms. When we nose a whiskey, we're trying to identify some of those compounds wafting off your glass. (Don't expect "subway platform" to appear in your whiskey, though.)

### No, That "Pear" You Smell Wasn't Infused into Your Whiskey

Notes like pear aren't physically added or infused into a whiskey. An aromatic molecule that smells like pear or banana can live in more places than just the physical fruit. In fact, a molecule that helps give pear its aroma can form as a happy by-product during the whiskey-making processes from grain to bottle, which I get into at length in chapter 2. I understand why this can be a confusing concept: Not only do we need to understand a wee bit of organic chemistry to fully grasp the idea, but many of you have seen vodka infusion jars sitting on a shelf behind your bartender, big chunks of pineapple, cinnamon sticks, or apples floating in them, dispersing flavor into the spirit. There is also a proliferation of "flavored" whiskeys on the market that add artificial or natural flavoring components like honey or cinnamon. Therefore, when I say, "Smell the banana and vanilla," the logical conclusion for some of you is that somewhere along the line someone infused in or added flavoring to the whiskey. So I'm not laughing at you when you ask me how whiskey is infused (I'm asked that all the time). I get it.

Here's how we get some of those flavors in whiskey, naturally, and using only those three ingredients—water, yeast, and grain. Let's say that seven carbon atoms, fourteen hydrogen atoms, and two oxygen atoms find one another and decide to hang out by forming bonds $(C_7H_{14}O_2)$. This organic molecular compound smells an awful lot like ripening fruit—perhaps a banana or pear. Scientists have given this molecule a very unromantic name: isoamyl acetate. Isoamyl acetate both evaporates off ripening fruit and can be coaxed out during the fermentation process involved in whiskey making (chapter 2). So when we talk about something smelling like "fruit" in a whiskey, what we may actually be smelling is the same molecular compound that is also found in a banana or pear.

In fact, thousands of compounds can combine to create just one smell. For example, when you smell a rose, you are enjoying close to thirteen hundred different molecular compounds configured in combinations of C, H, O, N, and S, each grouping elegantly dancing off the petals at different speeds—lithe, lighter molecules jump first. When you breathe in these compounds, they stimulate olfactory receptors that sit in your nasal cavity. Some receptors will react more strongly than others. In the blink of an eye, the activated receptors send a message to your brain, which in turn quietly whispers to you: "I am a rose."

Incidentally, some of the same molecules that create a rose scent also fly off a dram of whiskey, like the Glenmorangie Nectar D'or, for example, which is why you might say, "This smells floral." These feisty, smelly molecules—volatile molecules—bounce crazily all over your world. There could be as many as four hundred aromatic compounds in a whiskey.

## NOSING STARTS YOUNG, ATTRACTS CRAZIES

My precocious twelve-year-old niece once picked up a dram of whiskey I was drinking at a family gathering and said, "*Eeew*, this smells like rotten apple juice!" She was spot on. Some of the notes of that particular whiskey (Glenfiddich 12) are apples and pears. Is she a budding noser? Did she smell "fermentation"? I was once quoted in *Whisky Magazine* saying that enjoying Tullamore Dew 12 sort of reminded me of smelling and chewing paper in the first grade. That same year, *Wallpaper* magazine commissioned famed perfumer Geza Schoen to create a "perfume" called Paper Passion. Created with only five "woody" aromatic molecules, this wonderful concoction sold for $98 per bottle. I and a bunch of other crazies looked to snap it up.

### Don't Listen to Me Because I Don't Smell Like You Do

We have between 350 and 400 genes that determine our ability to receive and interpret smell. Approximately 150 of those genes, almost one third, show tremendous variability across the population. Some of us are blessed with fully functioning receptors, while others have small mutations that leave us unable to smell components of a molecule, or even the total molecular smell completely. This is called molecular "anosmia." Get this: *Every one of us has at least one specific anosmia.* If you happen to visit the Monell Center, one of the scientists there might demonstrate a little experiment for you by dousing artificial boar pheromones onto a small white strip and ask you to report what you nose. It's a popular and easy test that scientists use on subjects to explore variability. You might wince quickly, repulsed by the acrid boar odor, or you might report that it smells like nothing at all. A handful of you might say it smells slightly floral, and some of you will detect nothing at first, but over time, after repeated exposure, will develop sensitivity to the smell. That's variability.

When it comes to whiskey, there are probably hundreds of aromas that we all experience at different strengths and with different abilities, which means that learning how to trust and rely on your own palate and instinct is as important and valuable as considering an expert's judgment on a particular wine or whiskey. Two very popular aromas found in whiskey—sulfur and vanilla—are good examples of variability at work. Some of you will nose vanilla quite easily, while others will need large concentrations of vanilla for it to register. I'm particularly sensitive to sulfuric aromatics in a whiskey, and when it's present, the aromatic will overwhelm my senses. Some people don't smell it at all.

I was at a whiskey tasting recently when the distiller yelled, "Don't tell me you smell sulfur in my whiskey because it's not there!" Yet the sulfur note permeated many of the whiskeys he served. I stayed politely quiet, wondering if he had anosmia to the smell. The bottom line? It's okay to disagree. We all come to the table with a unique biological makeup and a distinct point of view. Here's something fascinating: Science shows our sense of smell is also highly malleable. You could already be a nosing and tasting genius, blessed with perfectly functioning receptors from your tongue to your cheeks to your nose. If you aren't, however, I have great news: Olfactory neurons are the only nerve cells in the body that regenerate—new ones replace the old every thirty to sixty days. Dr. Wysocki at Monell says that people who display anosmia to certain molecules can develop a sensitivity to them after exposing themselves a little bit every day for six weeks. So keep smiling!

## THE CULTURE OF SMELL

I've seen dozens of whiskey notes refer to "marzipan." When was the last time you had marzipan? How about the descriptors "sherrylike," or "Christmas cake"? I'm going to go out on a limb here and state boldly that 95 percent of people living outside the U.K. don't regularly drink sherry (though it's up and coming), don't serve Christmas fruitcakes on December 25, and never, ever break out marzipan over coffee. Save the queen's tongue and say a whiskey reminds you of an Almond Joy if it's true for you. Culturally speaking, we are not all on the same page.

## Aroma and Emotion

I mentioned earlier that aromas trigger a part of our brains that is closely linked to both emotion and memory. But how exactly? Lavender is thought to be a calming scent, but does it manipulate our brains in the same manner that a sedative might? Or does it trigger memories of a relaxing lavender bath we had when we were younger, which in turn relaxes us? In other words, do we have a biological response or a psychological one? And if we want to have a little fun with this, can we apply some of this research to our whiskey enjoyment? I think we can. If a memory comes to you while nosing and tasting a whiskey, pay attention to it—it is a fine way to describe what you are nosing. For example, you might say, "Something in this whiskey reminds me of Mom bringing a bowl full of fresh mint and herbs cut from her garden into the house." It may make you feel inexplicably happy or nostalgic. Go with it. Tell us all about it.

I recently held a class and served a "medicinal" whiskey along with some others on a tasting mat. "Medicinal" is one of the descriptors some whiskey tasters use to describe an aroma that falls under the heading of "phenolic compounds," a group of aromatic molecules that appear in whiskey while it sits in wood, or from the earthy peatiness burned during the process. For one of my students, the whiskey triggered memories of sickness and hospital visits. But another guy associated the smells with feeling clean and fresh, and he exclaimed, "I love this smell!" The response to aroma is deeply personal.

## YOU ARE YOUR OWN BEST WHISKEY EXPERT

With the human variability that exists when we nose and taste, how much stock can we put into an "expert" opinion or rating scale when it comes to whiskey or wine? I'm implicating myself here, but I also want to be honest about what I know to be true—I can guide you, but I can't tell you that you'll experience any given taste or aroma in exactly the same way as I do. And neither can any other whiskey expert. I've met experts on judging panels who smoke like fiends. A smoke-coated palate influences a whiskey experience, as do stress, coffee, gum, time of day, weather, and even music. No palate is the gold standard, and no one tastes quite like you do. Also, when you read tasting notes from a magazine or see them displayed on shelves at a liquor store—these are called "shelf talkers" in the industry—take them with a grain of salt, not as fact.

## Practical Tips for Nosing

Whiskey is bottled at a minimum of 40 percent alcohol by volume (ABV). If you approach a whiskey like it's wine and stick your nose far into the wineglass to pick up the aromas, you will literally anesthetize the olfactory nerves. It would take approximately a half hour to get back into the game of nosing and tasting after that. As my good friend Sam "Dr. Whisky" Simmons explains: *"Approach whiskey as you would a fine woman walking by at a bar. She smells good, but you approach gently. Don't stick your nose in it right away. Do that and you just might get burned."*

Take notice of the size of the glass, too. This will clue you about how to approach the whiskey. If you're served a large rocks glass filled with ice, or a thimble-pour of a light whiskey, you can nose more deeply into the glass because the alcohol "burn" will be mitigated. But, proceed with caution when diving into a hefty amount of whiskey in a wide-nosed container. It won't take much to get all those aromas—and an alcohol sting—into your nose.

It's always best to do a gentle sweep under your nose at a safe distance to start getting a nice perfume off the whiskey. Move in closer if you can. I keep my mouth slightly open when I nose so that air comes in simultaneously through my mouth—sort of the reverse smoker's trick.

After a while all this comes naturally—I can tell exactly where that good distance lies under my nose to get those nice aromatic compounds flowing toward me. You'll get there, too, and if you are at home with your own glassware (see chapter 4 for my recommendations), then even better—you are in control of the pour and the vessel.

Congratulations! You now know my biggest trade secret of all, one that already sets you way ahead of the game. Anyone who's ever attended my classes knows it, and now you know it: *Smell is the single most important element in evaluating and appreciating whiskey.* You were born to do this.

## Whiskey's Third Component (Beyond Taste and Smell)

The whiskey lord giveth and he taketh away. While the high alcohol content might take away our ability to detect subtlety on taste alone, it triggers something else, the same sensation that pleases lovers of spicy wings, hot phaal curry (or even spankings): Our trigeminal nerve is stimulated. The trigeminal nerve has nothing to do with smell or taste. It's the nerve that sends a message to our brain that says "pain" or "heat" or "cold." Chile peppers, wasabi, and mustard seeds all send messages of heat, and whiskey gives heat in spades. Other whiskeys stimulate our triggered nerve with a cooling message. At Monell we tasted WhistlePig Rye 10—an American whiskey that I often describe as "minty." As we exhaled after taking a sip, I felt that familiar cooling sensation on my tongue. Sensory psychologist Paul Wise says that when our trigeminal nerve is triggered, it doesn't result in taste, but rather a feeling, and in this case, it was a cooling feeling. Alcohol's effect on the trigeminal nerve, combined with rich aromatics, adds complexity to the overall perception of a whiskey.

As you taste your first whiskeys, observe any cooling or heating sensations, too. I like whiskey with a "kick," especially on cold nights, but I don't like it to overwhelm my senses so much that my eyes water, because in that case I truly do become irritated. Balance is key.

### Whiskey Color

After you spend time nosing a whiskey, pull the glass back and hold your whiskey to the light—from gold to deep russet, a whiskey's color can reveal valuable information. Darker, ruby-esque colors generally indicate that it's an older whiskey, while if there's a light golden or straw hue, it's likely younger. The type of wood in which a whiskey ages, and the techniques whiskey makers practice to marry casks together (called vatting), influence color as well.

Some whiskey companies will use caramel coloring (also called E150a in Europe), making it trickier for us to evaluate age on color alone. They'd never reveal it, but hundreds of distilleries worldwide use some coloring, even if it's just a trace amount. Caramel shouldn't change the flavor of your whiskey, but personally I can't wait until this practice becomes obsolete, and for all of us to get used to seeing color variations in our bottles. However, many whiskey companies think a rich color is more appealing to consumers. Let me tell you here: A darker color does not always mean a higher quality whiskey. I once tasted a delicious, rich, and very rare bottle of Glenfiddich 50 Years Old Scotch that sells for about $33,000 a bottle. You'd never have guessed that it was aged for fifty years by looking at the light and pretty golden hue reflecting off my glass.

American whiskey regulations are stricter than Scottish regulations regarding caramel color. Any American whiskey with the word "straight" listed on the bottle does not contain any coloring. ("Straight" simply means the whiskey was aged for a minimum of two years—I'll get into this more when we talk about American whiskeys in chapter 3.) In Scotland, any whisky producer can use E150a to harmonize the color of whiskey. In fact, the majority of blended Scotch whiskies and many single malt Scotch whiskies—the two most popular styles of Scotch sold worldwide—contain some caramel coloring.

My biggest pet peeve with regard to coloring is when it comes to whiskeys that are considered rare or exclusive. If I find out that a small amount of coloring has been used, I feel a bit duped, even though rationally I don't think I'd taste the difference without it. A recent move toward eliminating this practice in Scotland, prompted no doubt by conversations online among whiskey geeks and critics, is well under way, though. Here's a tip: Should you speak any German and are absolutely dying to compile your own list of colored versus noncolored whiskey, the German regulations require a bottle to list whether or not color is added. Otherwise, don't worry too much about it right now because in the grand scheme of things, it won't affect your whiskey enjoyment when it comes to nosing and tasting. Still, I want you to know about how that color may get in there.

## WHAT IS A DRAM ANYWAY?

Bob Dylan sings, "The whole world's a bottle / And life's but a dram." Essentially, a dram is a small amount of something—technically speaking, a unit of apothecary weight of one eighth of a fluid ounce, or historically, sixty grains. Dylan didn't mean to get too literal and your bartender won't be so literal either. Most likely he or she will pour whatever looks like just enough liquid to satisfy both the bottom line and your palate without complaint. The etymology of the word, in case you are curious, most likely comes from the word *drachma*, meaning "measure of weight" and also "silver coin" in Greek. It also happens to be the basic monetary unit of Armenia, so if you order a dram there, you are asking for some cold, hard cash and not whiskey.

## Whiskey to the Lips! Mouthfeel, Body, and Finish

After you nose a few times, and make a few mental notes about the aroma while taking in the color, go ahead and take your first sip. Whiskey is to be savored and enjoyed, so notice I didn't say, "Take a *shot*." Simply sip the same amount you might with a glass of your favorite wine. Now you get to *taste*, and the taste will blossom because you've honored your nose. The aromas will bounce around your mouth and up through the back of your nasal cavity after you swallow. You might find some hidden aromatic gems you may not have noticed when you were first tasting it.

As you taste, notice how the whiskey feels on your tongue, roof of your mouth, and toward the back of your tongue. The dominant taste sensations are sweet, bitter, salty, and umami. Do you notice any bitter sensations? How about some sweetness somewhere? How does the sensation of sweet on your tongue interact with what you've nosed to create an overall flavor? Any saltiness? Any alcohol tingling? Did you feel any of the cooling or warming sensations I talked about earlier? Hold the whiskey in your mouth for ten seconds before swallowing—what did you notice? Ask yourself about the texture of the whiskey—we refer to this most often as the "mouthfeel." Is it creamy? Oily-ish? Thin? How about the weight of it? Does it feel full and heavy? Steal wine's use of the word "body" if you want to, as in "This is a full-bodied whiskey." You'll start to notice different mouthfeels and different bodies among whiskeys once you get going.

### WHISKEY FACTS DISTILLED

**MOUTHFEEL:** Refers to the texture of a whiskey in your mouth. Words like "creamy," "oily," "thin," and "rich" are the most common descriptors for a whiskey's mouthfeel.

**BODY:** Refers to the fullness or weight of the whiskey in your mouth.

**FINISH:** Refers to the texture, notes, and feel of the whiskey that remain noticeable after you swallow it.

After you swallow, make a note of how long the flavor lingers. This is called the "finish." Finish simply refers to the final impression a whiskey leaves on your palate. Does it stay for a long time? That would be a long finish. Did you like the long finish? Call that a nice, long finish. Sometimes new notes burst along the finish, too. Coffee, chocolate, and some of those tannic or woody notes I'll describe soon often develop and linger along the finish. Some whiskeys barely have any finish at all, disappearing altogether the moment you swallow.

Older whiskeys tend to have a longer finish than younger whiskeys do. It's something many whiskey pros look for in an aged or vintage whiskey. But a long finish isn't always the mark of a better whiskey or one that's right for the drinking occasion. Sometimes I like a thinner whiskey that rapidly disappears as an aperitif, especially during warm spring months.

### Should You "Swirl" Your Whiskey? Chew? Spit?

You may have seen whiskey or wine pros swirl their glasses before taking a taste. Go ahead and do the same thing, but you don't need to get too crazy or uptight about it. A few swift circular movements at most will do. A little motion will encourage more aromatic molecules to waft up toward your nose. Sometimes I swirl and sometimes I don't, depending on my mood. If I'm truly evaluating a whiskey, I'll give it a whirl. Otherwise, I sit at a bar and just chill out with my glass without any hoopla.

A lot of experts do something with their mouths called the Kentucky chew when they evaluate a whiskey. It involves sipping, then "chewing" it around your mouth, while inhaling through your nose. When you do this, you're supposed to make a sound that sounds like *num-num* with your tongue and lips. I find the Kentucky chew quite goofy and distracting in public, and for me it's not so necessary. Yet if I'm truly judging a whiskey quietly at home or on a panel, I'll inhale gently, with my mouth slightly open, and let air flow over the whiskey on my tongue. An open mouth helps me feel the heating and cooling sensations as I breathe in and out.

Remember, whiskey is very high in alcohol by volume, so depending on how much you plan to taste, you may need to spit your whiskey. You won't get the full whiskey experience, but you also won't find yourself lying facedown in the front yard later, either.

## ADDING WATER TO WHISKEY?

At the Scotch Malt Whisky Society in Edinburgh where I worked, glass pitchers of water are placed on the long library tables for guests who like to add water to their whisky—which is a good number. In the United States, though, Scotch lovers in particular tell me what blasphemy it is to add water. Just do it. Add water if you want to. Adding water is yet another way to express aromatics and flavors of a whiskey—you'll essentially change which characteristics pop or stay quiet. I'll try water on any type of whiskey, whether that's Japanese, American, or Scottish, and see what happens. Many evaluators who serve on tasting panels with me dilute their whiskey with half as much water to find what my friend Ian Millar says are the "hidden distillery characteristics." My advice? Be careful. As Ian says, "You can add it, but you cannae take it away." A few drops in your dram should suffice if you are curious. Don't feel compelled either way.

If you've read this far, you've made it! I've shared with you all the steps I use myself when I taste a whiskey, tips that I hope you'll use when you go through your first tasting at the end of this chapter.

## WHY THE HECK IS HE RUBBING HIS HANDS WITH THAT WHISKEY?

I've been to tastings and seen the whiskey professor or distiller take some whiskey, rub it in his hands, and enjoy a nice big whiff. You'll come across this practice, too, so I thought I'd let you know what's going on. Like perfume, the aromatics in a whiskey will react to the heat on human skin, so when you put whiskey on your hands and rub your hands together, you can release aromas. I once received a gift of a tiny but elegant little French perfume bottle of pure single malt Scotch from an artist. I spray it on the single ladies at the bar where I work and let the men come flocking.

## BUILDING YOUR LIST OF DESCRIPTORS

With all the variability and subjectivity there is when it comes to experiencing whiskey, you might wonder how we can say anything universal at all about whiskey. Don't fret. There are a few notes that most people—novices and experts alike—often experience. In this section, I'll explain the characteristics many whiskeys share—a "greatest hits list" of aromatic, taste, and mouthfeel descriptors. I don't want you to get totally hung up on assigning words to your whiskey, though. Remember, that task may interfere with your sensory appreciation. Fact: If you're *lucky*, you'll be able to identify four or five aromatics in each whiskey. I know a few whiskey writers and reviewers who won't be happy to hear that: They've got careers built on publishing laundry lists of aromatic descriptors in giant encyclopedic books. But here's another secret Dr. Rachel Herz shared with me: Professors, chefs, sommeliers, perfumers, and other top-notch nosers can't pick more than three to five aromas out of a mixture. Whiskey is a mixture. So don't pressure yourself to find a bazillion smells.

General characteristics will spring to mind when you taste a whiskey, whether it's sweet or spicy, for example. Don't silence those impressions; instead, follow the chart below and try to dig a little deeper and build a more detailed whiskey vocabulary. Your mind will start flowing and you'll combine flavors to make new ones, that is, almond + vanilla + chocolate + coconut = Almond Joy. If you can get five aromatics on smell alone, that's great.

## WHISKEY TASTING VOCABULARY BASICS

**NOSE:** Aromatic notes picked up by the nasal receptors located in your nasal cavity. The aroma of a whiskey can pass by the receptors either during inhalation (orthonasal olfaction) or exhalation (retronasal olfaction).

**TASTE OR PALATE:** The combination of what we perceive on the tongue with the information we get while nosing and exhaling during and after sipping.

**FLAVOR:** The descriptor used to describe the overall experience: the taste, nose, and overall physical sensory experience.

## TABLE 1: THE WHISKEY DESCRIPTOR GREATEST HITS LIST

| WHEN YOU THINK . . . TO YOURSELF | YOU MIGHT WRITE OR SAY . . . |
|---|---|
| Sweet | Vanilla, Coconut, Almond, Cherry, Milk Chocolate, White Chocolate, Maple Syrup, Caramel, Toffee, Honey, Butterscotch, Marshmallow, Brown Sugar, Molasses |
| Woody | Pine, Cedar, Oak, Sawdust, Tannin, Black Tea, Banana Peel, Citrus Rind, Dark Chocolate, Coffee, Leather, Tobacco |
| Spice | Cloves, Cinnamon, Anise, Nutmeg, Pepper |
| Floral | Lavender, Rose, Geranium, Cut Flowers |
| Fruity | Apple, Pear, Peach, Banana, Apricot, Fig, Raisin, Lemon, Lime, Orange |
| Green | Hay, Mowed Grass, Herbaceous |
| Smoke | Campfire, Wood Fire, BBQ |
| Egg, Rubber | Sulfur |
| Peat | Iodine, Medicinal, Band-Aids |
| Nutty | Walnut, Hazelnut, Pecan |
| Heat/Sting | Mustard Seeds, Wasabi, Chile Peppers, Higher ABV |
| Cool/Sting | Menthol, Mint, Spearmint, Peppermint, Higher ABV |
| The flavor didn't last too long. | This is an approachable, light whiskey. |
| This filled my entire mouth with flavor. | This is a robust, rich whiskey. |
| This whiskey coats my mouth and lingers there. | This is an oily whiskey. |
| This whiskey is silky and easy. | This is a creamy whiskey. |
| This burns. | What a long, warm finish. |
| This whiskey is "winey." | This might be a sherried whiskey. |

## SWEET

Sweet is technically not an aroma. It is a *taste* descriptor. When you smell something and think to yourself "sweet," challenge yourself by quietly asking, "What kind of sweet?" Is it sweet like milk chocolate? Sweet like cake? Often, popular whiskey aromatic notes such as coconut, vanilla, caramel, florals, and brown sugar come across as sweet on the nose—and with reason. Most of the time when we smell vanilla, a sweet taste will accompany our expectations of it, so we describe its smells as sweet. After tasting your whiskey, a sweet impression on the nose might explode the aromas into something more grand—look for combinations of spice, citrus, vanilla, coconut, or chocolate working together with the sensation of sweet on your tongue to create a wonderful combination. You may be reminded of sweet treats like a delicious homemade pie or the Almond Joy bar I mentioned earlier.

### Vanilla

When a spirit sits in wood casks over time, it grabs flavorful molecules out of the wood and intermingles with it. Vanilla is one of the most common notes that a cask imparts to a whiskey. Vanilla may have been the very first flavor you were exposed to in life—mother's milk contains the compound—and exists in so many places in nature that it would be impossible to count them all here. By now you have experienced this aroma in everything from cookies to soaps, so teasing this flavor out of your dram will be one of the easier tasks, especially when it comes to American whiskeys. The brand-new oak casks (virgin casks) that American whiskey makers use to age whiskey release an incredible influx of vanilla notes into the spirit very quickly, so search for this aroma as you explore American whiskeys especially. You can find vanilla in whiskeys from all other regions as well; however, a majority of whiskeys produced outside the United States are aged in what we call "refill" or "seasoned" casks, meaning that spirit or wine has already been aged within it (more on this in chapter 3). The vanilla notes will be subtler.

To practice identifying vanilla, grab a bottle of pure vanilla extract from your cupboard and hold the extract in one hand, whiskey in the other, and nose them side by side. This is a great way to identify flavors in your glass, and exactly what I did for years as I practiced.

## Coconut

The heavy, rich coconut aroma in whiskey comes from a class of molecules called lactones, which exist in wood casks. Again, American whiskey is full of this aroma because the lactones are some of the first notes a spirit pulls out of fresh, new American oak. Wine extracts lactones from casks as well, so your favorite wine may have this note, but in more subtle amounts. Scotch can deliver a slight coconut aroma, too, and I find the note most often in younger Scotch or in Scotch that has been aged in brand-new casks like an American whiskey. Glenmorangie 10 (a young Scotch) and Glenfiddich 15 (uses new American oak for aging) are two single malt Scotch whiskies that deliver coconut aromatics.

## Caramel/Coffee/Toffee

Barley is one of the most popular grains around the world used to create whiskey—especially in Scotland, Ireland, and Japan. Barley sugars generate an organic substance called furfurals—a family of compounds that emit the caramel/toffee/coffee notes you will encounter. The word "furfural" actually derives from the Latin word *furfur*, which means "bran." Some have likened the aromatic note to almonds, too. Like so many whiskey notes, these notes can also come from the cask.

## MAPLE SYRUP

You may likely say "This smells like a pancake!" after sipping American whiskey. Let me be the first to share with you that the molecule soloton, which can arise out of wood after it's charred on the inside with flame—a practice used by whiskey makers to condition casks for aging—is also a compound that is found naturally in maple syrup. Don't live in the northeastern United States or Canada, where maple syrup flows plentifully? No worries—Aunt Jemima carries a synthetic version of soloton in her belly, too. So double fist some maple syrup and whiskey to see if you can't conjure up "pecan pie" or "breakfast." Both are perfectly acceptable dram descriptors.

## WOODY

I am seduced by aromatic notes that evoke images of plump, leathery mahogany club chairs, stuffed deer heads, and tobacco-faded books lined up neatly in an oak case. I imagine a place with this old-world aristocratic charm and the masculine aromas that often fall under the "woody" category: oak, leather, pine, tobacco, cedar. Like "sweet," "woody" is another umbrella term that describes a cornucopia of related notes that I find very evocative, too—"woody" can smell like a cozy log cabin or remind you of riding a bike on a tree-lined bike path in Cape Cod. Look to your own experiences for some of those notes when you think "woody." Woody aromatic notes come from the cask in which a whiskey has been aged, as you can probably guess. On the tongue, you may experience the effects of wood as "bitter" or "strong." You'll sense the wood mostly toward the back and sides of your tongue, even though we have receptors all over our mouths to receive them. The bitterness often comes from what we call tannins—for example, that drying or puckering bitterness you taste in black tea, a sliver of orange rind, or a banana peel are caused by tannins. Tannins are also present on grape skins, pips, and stems, which means that you've probably used this term extensively if you are a wine aficionado. I think a dose of tannin in just the right amounts helps a whiskey develop complexity and delivers what I call a "backbone." Without tannins, some whiskeys would be too cloying. Look for different types of woody notes and varying tannic sensations coming from the wood on the tongue in every whiskey you taste—they're in there.

## SPICE

The spice you nose may very well come from a molecule called eugenol. Almost 80 percent of cloves are made up of this molecule, so when your brain says "clove," you probably smell this compound. Basil, rosemary, pineapples, cinnamon, mangoes, and apples contain some amounts of eugenol, although to a lesser extent. As you look for a spice note in your whiskey, see if you can identify the clove element in particular. "Nutmeg," "allspice," and "cinnamon" are also very popular descriptors in whiskey. Run through those words as you nose and see if any pop.

## FLORAL

A mishmash of floral notes reminiscent of rose, lavender, geranium, lemongrass, and lily of the valley come from two categories of compounds: terpenes and esters. In whiskey speak, you'll mostly hear whiskey makers talking of esters or an "estery" spirit, by which they mostly mean that the whiskey contains a slew of these light floral or citrus notes—sometimes both. Many of these pretty aromatics form before whiskey is even put into a cask, specifically during fermentation and distillation. I'll excite you with the art and science distillers use to make your favorite dram in chapter 2.

### IMPORTANT ANNOUNCEMENT: OLDER WHISKEY DOES NOT MEAN BETTER WHISKEY!

Go ahead, be shocked. But it's true. As a whiskey sits in a cask, over time softer aromas such as lemon and rose become harder to detect because deeper and richer cask notes like tobacco, leather, and spice can ripen and overpower the subtlety of a flower or fresh summery fruit. You may discover a weakness for light, *younger* whiskeys. Light whiskeys can be very refreshing, like sipping a glass of cool lemonade or rose hip iced tea on a hot day. If light and fruity agrees with your palate, count yourself among the many whiskey fans who would choose to bring along a young whiskey if they were stranded on a desert island.

### Fruity

Mmmmm . . . apples, pears, limes, lemons, oranges, peaches, and blackberries are some of the mouthwatering fruits I love to identify in a whiskey. Fruity elements like these also fall under the "ester" heading—aromatic compounds created mostly during fermentation and distillation that are often silenced by wood over time. Fruity qualities—and floral for that matter—do not mean that a whiskey will necessarily taste sweet. You've probably tasted a sauvignon blanc wine that delivered notes of fruits on the nose yet still remained tart and tingly on the tongue. This juxtaposition happens in whiskey, too: The whiskey might nose fruity but deliver a nice big, dry mouthfeel.

There are also some fruity notes that are commonly associated with wood as well, so when you taste them, you'll know the reason they're in your glass. Some of those players are figs, raisins, and prunes.

### Green

Hay, grass, and heather are all "green" characteristics, for lack of a better word—think running through an open field, breathing in the fresh air. These are notes often born in the whiskey-making process before aging occurs. Some whiskeys have a fresh soap quality in the nose. Interestingly, one of the common molecules in whiskey that emits a "green" smell is called coumarin (also an ester) and has been used to enhance scent in beauty products since the late 1800s. Lemongrass contains some coumarin, as do sweet grass and many other plants. That's why you might experience some whiskeys as "clean, fresh, and green." I think that many young, nonpeated, nonsherried single malt Scotch whiskies have this quality.

## Oily

The presence of natural fatty acids or lipids—types of molecules—contributes to an oily or viscous whiskey texture. Fatty acids can develop both in the distillation process and during casking. Look for this quality especially in whiskeys labeled as "non-chill filtered." Many whiskey makers choose to leave fatty acids and lipids (and sediment, too) in the whiskey, while others take it out through a filtration process. (I'll tell you why a distiller might choose to chill filter a whiskey or not, and how it does it, when we dig deeper into whiskey making in chapter 2.)

## Rich

Older whiskeys—single malt Scotches in particular—can become rich and thick as they approach the quarter-century mark. Water evaporates off the whiskey over time, leaving a liquid with a higher alcohol content in its place. High alcohol content gives whiskey a more syrupy texture. I also find that whiskeys aged in casks that once held sherry will impart notes like fig, cocoa, raisin, and leather into a whiskey—prompting me to use the word "rich" when I taste them, too. Very old whiskeys that have been aged in sherry butts are some of the richest whiskeys you'll ever taste—many types of Scotch are aged in old sherry casks. This is not to say that there aren't some thick and rich whiskeys made in other regions—rich whiskey can be found in any region and "rich" is a word you can use for any whiskey that strikes you as such.

## Creamy

I use "creamy" to describe a milky, silky texture that pleasantly coats my mouth, and often accompanies lighter aromatics like citrus, vanillas, and florals. Many Irish whiskeys taste very creamy to me, as do Japanese whiskies. I visited one Japanese distiller who explained to me that creaminess comes from *Lactobacillus* bacteria, which produce lactic acid and find their way into a cask during fermentation. These same lactic acids are also found in yogurt and cheese. While you wouldn't want the sour taste of yogurt and cheese in your whiskey, a distiller who can tweak and use *Lactobacillus* effectively will also make a nicely textured whiskey—Yamazaki 12, a Japanese whisky, comes to mind when I think of a creamy texture.

## Sulfur

Not everyone experiences the intensity of a sulfur-y spirit the same way. Some palates are way more sensitive to picking up this quality in a whiskey, or wine for that matter. Many people experience anosmia when it comes to sulfuric aromas such as "pencil" or "burned rubber." Personally, I am not partial to the sulfurlike aromas some whiskeys exhibit because I am very sensitive to them. To me, sulfur has too strong of an egg note, like something is "off." It's the smell at my car mechanic's while I'm waiting for him to change my tires. I try not to get too vocal about my dislike for the sulfur notes of some whiskeys, however. Once, during an evaluation of a major distillery's cask sample that was not yet bottled for the consumer market, I described the display of aromas as like a "rotten egg." Another whiskey expert sitting next to me described it as "wonderful, earthy, barnyard, mushroom-y." So, to each his or her own. You'll identify more earthy, sulfuric notes in whiskeys aged in old sherry casks, which often give off this note along with some of the more pleasant ones like fig, raisin, and dark cherry.

## PEAT AND SMOKE

### Peat (Stop Using That Word Until You Read This, Please!)

The word "peat" is bandied about so often on bar stools, in classes, and by so many of the branded whiskey ambassadors I know—without explanation or demonstration—that it has now become virtually synonymous with Scotch whisky, even though only about 10 percent of distilleries in Scotland produce what we call a "peated" whiskey. Japan and India, and even a few brave American whiskey makers, now make a peated-style whiskey, but for the most part when you identify peat in your whiskey, assume it comes from Scotland.

First, let's start with what peat actually is. Peat is partially decayed organic material made mostly of plants. In Scotland, the wet, oceanic climate creates a nice environment for peat to form because the water levels hinder oxygen's ability to totally break down plant matter or, in other words, to let it fully decay. This partially decayed, dark, soft earth covers almost 23 percent of the Scottish landscape and in some places reaches close to twenty-six feet deep. Also called moors or muskegs, these grand swaths of landscape made of peat contain heathers, mosses, and various grasses. Don't get confused here about the smell of peat—because these plants are decaying, that's quite a different smell from the "green" notes I referred to earlier, which have more of the "I'm running through a summer field" smell.

For hundreds (thousands) of years, populations in the tree-barren landscape of the northern Celtic regions dried peat into chunks called briquettes, lighting them to heat their homes and to cook. Peat is now most famously associated with distilleries based on the Scottish island called Islay, where distillers there light it to dry wet barley during a process we call malting (more mention of malting in chapter 2). Peat and smoke notes infuse the moist barley and will dramatically change the aromatic profile of the eventual whiskey. Burning peat actually transports its strong-smelling compounds into the barley along with smoke, and they remain there throughout the whiskey-making process. The concentration of peat in a whiskey is measured in what is called parts per million (ppm), and a trend now is to list the ppm on the bottle like a badge of honor and beacon for peat lovers.

After many years, I can finally detect peat like a champ. It often comes hand in hand with a smoky aroma, but it is distinctly different from smoke. Smoke is . . . well . . . *smoke*. You know what smoke smells like. I would describe peat as "medicinal" or "iodinelike." I am often impressed when a whiskey virgin says, "Sorry, this just smells like Band-Aids or disinfectant to me." That person's nosing ability is ace. Cresol, a synthetic replica of a compound found naturally in peat, is used in deodorants, Band-Aids, and even Sharpies.

## PEAT IS AN ECOLOGICAL ISSUE

Various kinds of peat are found throughout the world. Peat has a tremendous capacity to store carbon dioxide, which makes harvesting it somewhat of a controversial subject now. Climate specialists claim that the layers of peat around the world are as important to world ecology as the rain forests. Peat is not generally considered a renewable source of energy, even though it can technically renew itself very slowly. Bogs take thousands of years to develop and grow at about a half an inch per century.

Some of you will become peat fanatics when you first experience it (you may be already). At the end of the Scotch section in chapter 3, I'll provide you with a peated whiskey list, organized by ppm, so that you can host your own peat party.

## THE *FINISH* LINE

We're *almost* there. Now that you know the basics of nosing and tasting, it's time to start nosing and tasting.

### YOU'LL LOVE WHISKEY NUMBER 3!

As you approach the third or fourth whiskey in a tasting, the whiskeys miraculously become "smooth." Your brain, tongue, and nose already know what to expect and are fully prepared for the experience. You adapt. The first whiskey offered up in a tasting is at a clear disadvantage, and so I am always rearranging my whiskey-tasting glass arrangements to get a better picture of a taster's feelings about a particular whiskey brand or style. When a new student exclaims that "number 1" in a lineup is his or her favorite, I know it's a winner! Change the order of your whiskey tasting with friends with this in mind.

### Putting It All Together in Your First Flight: The Broad Tasting

The first whiskey tasting is designed to help you explore classic styles from the big whiskey-producing regions: Scotland, Ireland, America, and Japan. I call this a "whiskey tasting in broad strokes," and I host broad tastings regularly at The Flatiron Room. Once you've discovered a few whiskeys that pique your curiosity, you'll probably want to explore one style more deeply and spend time uncovering the nuances among a bunch of bourbons or single malt Scotches. The more similar the styles, the more challenging it is to discuss and identify how the whiskeys are distinct. Think of it this way: Imagine yourself at the hardware store choosing among different shades of white for your bedroom wall color. You've already narrowed down that of all the thousands of paint options across the color spectrum, you like white. But then, you'll need to shuffle through a slew of paint chips with names like linen, cream, alabaster, oyster, pearl, and lily to figure out which you like best, only the differences are very subtle. This tasting is a broad tasting to help you narrow down whiskeys by their more obvious characteristics so that you can experience their more subtle differences later on.

Remember, there are no right or wrong answers when it comes to what you like. I was once quoted in *The New York Times* for touting Hudson Baby Bourbon as a nice summertime dram, and then got hounded on Twitter by a couple of whiskey freaks who said that Hudson wasn't any good and that I had no taste. Never listen to that kind of criticism. I don't. But a little friendly debate among friends is fine.

Use the descriptors I've given you as a base to help you describe the aromas. Remember, an aroma may also spark a memory—just go with whatever associations pop into your mind. For example, whiskeys remind me of musicians a lot. Really, the sky's the limit. Get creative. Whatever it takes to help you loosen up and have a good time.

### Getting the Bottles

I recommend gathering a group of friends together for this tasting so you can split bottle costs. I'll give you a whiskey shopping list on pages 41–43, and you can choose one of the options under each region listed for the tasting. This list, and all the lists in this book, is based on widespread availability, value, and what I'd call good-quality liquid. The cool thing about whiskey is that you won't—and shouldn't—finish the bottles in one night. Unlike wine, the whiskey won't age or "turn" within a few days—or even within the next year. You can buy some flasks online or small empty bottles (aka jars) from a kitchen store like Williams-Sonoma with blank labels so you can add handwritten notes. You can split the leftover whiskey among the group. Keep in mind that what might seem like a hefty investment initially is actually no more expensive than many wine tastings, per glass. You can use the whiskey to make some great cocktails, too (see chapter 5).

---

## SCIENTIFIC RATIONALE FOR A WHISKEY TASTING IN BROAD CONTRASTS

We adapt to certain smells and tastes, a trait called "human adaptability." Our palate is wired to detect change, so if you taste six whiskeys of a similar style side by side, each releasing a coconut note, that note stops standing out. You will notice only what is different in the next glass. Most tastings conducted by whiskey experts for judging are grouped by similar styles. Could one whiskey actually neutralize another? I rotate my tasting order often and am a huge fan of the broad whiskey tasting for this reason.

---

### Broad Tasting Guidelines

Choose one in each category. You should be able to find most brands at your local store—I didn't include small craft brands or pricey brands that can be hard to find (though we'll get into some of those later). Also, you'll see some categories have more choices than others; this is simply because there are more on offer. I don't recommend any whiskeys I don't like or wouldn't drink myself.

### AMERICAN WHISKEY: BOURBON
Four Roses Yellow Label or Single Barrel
Buffalo Trace Bourbon
Elijah Craig 12
Old Grand-Dad

Eagle Rare
Woodford Reserve
Evan Williams Single Barrel
Michter's Bourbon
Old Forrester Signature Reserve

**American Whiskey: Rye**
Rittenhouse Rye
Knob Creek Rye
Wild Turkey Rye
Russell's Reserve Rye 6

**Single Malt Scotch: Nonpeated, Nonsmoked**
Glenmorangie 10
Glenfiddich 12
The Balvenie 12 DoubleWood
Auchentoshan Three Wood
GlenDronach 12
Scapa 16
Macallan Fine Oak 15

**Irish Whiskey**
Tullamore Dew 10
Redbreast 12
Bushmills 10
Knappogue Castle 12

**Single Malt Scotch: Smoke, Peat**
Laphroaig 10
Ardbeg 10
Bowmore 12
Highland Park 12

JAPANESE WHISKY
Yamazaki 12 (single malt)
Nikka 12 (slightly peated, pure malt)
Hakushu 12 (slightly peated, single malt)
Hibiki 12 (blend)

IF YOU CAN'T FIND JAPANESE WHISKY OR ARE MORE CURIOUS
ABOUT BLENDED SCOTCH, ADD ONE OF THE FOLLOWING INSTEAD
Blended Scotch
Dewar's 12
Johnnie Walker Black Label
Chivas Regal 12

## HOW TO CONDUCT YOUR TASTING

1. Set up your glasses in a row from left to right.
2. Pour about ½ ounce whiskey into each glass in this order: 1. Irish whiskey. 2. Single malt Scotch, nonpeated. 3. Japanese whisky or blend. 4. Bourbon. 5. Rye. 6. Big smoky Scotch. The tasting order moves from light-style whiskeys to more robust whiskeys.
3. Gently pick up glass number 1 and pull it toward your nose.
4. Swirl your glass lightly, then nose again.
5. Check out the color.
6. While holding number 1 (Irish) in your left hand, pick up whiskey number 6 (smoked/peated) in your right. Nose them back-to-back. Notice the big difference between them.
7. Put number 6 (smoked/peated) down without tasting it. Now pick up whiskey number 4 (bourbon) and do the same thing, comparing it with number 1 (Irish) as well. Make some observations.

8.  Now that you've got your nose and brain "warmed up," put down number 1 and start playing with your whiskey. Nose the two American whiskeys together. Nose the bourbon against the nonpeated Scotch.

9.  Keep pulling different whiskeys toward your nose—randomly is fine—until you feel as if you've got their personalities down, and start making mental notes as to which whiskey you are most excited to taste based on aroma. You're now beginning to develop a whiskey opinion.

10. Taste them. I'd start from left to right, tasting them all *except* whiskey number 6. The peat/smoke element will coat your mouth and change the way you experience the other whiskeys, so save this for last, and for when you are done tasting all the other whiskeys.

11. Start tasting and notice the texture of different whiskeys. Look for that retronasal olfaction—the aromas that reach your olfactory receptors from your mouth as you inhale while eating and drinking. Finally, how is each finish different?

12. Keep playing by nosing and tasting all the whiskeys in different combinations.

13. Jot down a few aromatics and taste descriptors that come to mind.

14. Think about which whiskeys you like best—you might like one best on the nose, but like a different one on the overall palate once you taste them all. That's perfectly reasonable.

15. Pat yourself on the back—you've now started developing your whiskey palate!

# 2

# Whiskey Making = Flavor Making!

*From Grain to Bottle*

FEELING COMFORTABLE WITH YOUR nose and building your whiskey vocabulary make you a better whiskey consumer. But if you are anything like I am, you want to know more. You want to get into the nitty-gritty of how whiskey is made. You want to know how that flavor gets into the liquid.

I don't have a chemistry degree. I can't actually distill whiskey nor can I build a barrel. Still, I've devoured whiskey books, tasted every whiskey I could get my hands on at conferences and events, and stomped through distilleries in Europe, all over the U.S.A., and even Japan. Along the way, I learned why distillers do things like measure the gravity of distillate or cook grains at different temperatures in a mash tun, a large vat where grains are immersed with warm water. I once took a month-long leave of absence to live at a distillery. There, I tilled barley until blisters grew on my palms, threw anthracite clumsily into a malting kiln, and tasted whiskeys right out of a cask to help evaluate whether the "juice" was good enough to bottle. It was a completely magical experience. In this chapter, I'll do my best to seduce you with the art and science that are whiskey making. Sit in a comfortable chair with your favorite dram and let's get started.

## NO GRAIN? NO WHISKEY

We need starch to create whiskey. If you stopped for a moment and thought, *What exactly is a starch, anyway?*, you wouldn't be alone. Most people think of starch when it comes to food: pizza, cake, cookies, muffins—the tasty foods the doctor tells us we shouldn't eat in excess, but we do anyway.

A starch is a type of carbohydrate called a polysaccharide. Carbohydrates consist of carbon, hydrogen, and oxygen chains—the basic components of life, really (which makes "usquebaugh," the Gaelic word meaning "water of life," from which the word "whiskey" is derived, particularly apt). A polysaccharide is a longer chain consisting of many of those compounds, hence the word "poly," as in "polygamous," like Kublai Khan. The word "saccharide" means "sugar," and in biochemistry the word is actually used interchangeably with the word "carbohydrate." In wine making, grape sugars that occur during ripening are carbohydrates known as glucose and fructose—they are simpler, lighter monosaccharides. But whiskey uses those nice big long-chain compounds, which come in the form of grains.

Without a starch source, we can't make whiskey, wine, or any other type of alcoholic spirit. We need those sugars not only to help nurture the development of flavor components, but also to actually put the alcohol into your alcohol with the help of a little yeast, which feeds off of those sugars. That's what fermentation is. But I'm already getting ahead here. Allow me to introduce you to the four most popular grains used in whiskey production: barley, corn, rye, and wheat.

---

### WHISKEY DISTILLED FACT

*Without a starch source, we can't make whiskey, wine, or any other type of alcoholic spirit. To make wine, we use grapes. For tequila, it's agave. To make whiskey, we use grains—predominantly barley, corn, rye, and wheat. Each grain variant contributes to a whiskey's flavor and identity.*

---

Often referred to as the "mash bill," the types and varying percent-ages of grain used to make a whiskey contribute to the overall flavor. You'll start to notice the word "mash bill" pop up mostly with American whiskey. American whiskeys play with all the dominant grains in order to create flavor. American bourbon, for example, must include 51 per-cent corn in the mash bill, but the other 49 percent is up for grabs. Scotland, Japan, and Ireland are often barley loyalists, and some types of whiskeys produced in these countries are even restricted by law to in-clude 100 percent barley. Single malt Scotch, for example, must be 100 percent barley (we'll talk a lot more about single malts in chapter 3). When you see the word "malt" on a whiskey label anywhere in the world, your mind should immediately think "barley."

### Malted Barley

We need to extract fermentable sugars from the grain to create alcohol and flavor for our whiskey—how we extract the sugars from barley begins with the process of malting. (Note: Some Irish whiskeys use unmalted barley.) Here's how it works and why it's needed: Barley = polysaccharide = a type of carbohydrate = sugar, all bound up inside a little seed. The seed stores those sugars to protect itself and conserve energy for when it's needed. The trick is to get at those sugars—and eventually flavors.

Malting is the process by which barley is tricked into germination and then dried into a crispy little seed so that the full plant can't grow. Enzymes developed during malting do two things: First, they break down little protein walls inside the seeds into a form that yeast can eat, and second, they change the starches into sugars. Because malted barley is such a good little sugar-making catalyst, many whiskey makers will use small percentages of barley to facilitate that conversion.

Chocolate, biscuits, and malty are all notes commonly associated with barley. But personally, I don't like using the word "malty" because

I don't think too many people know what malty actually smells like, or even means. That's not a bad thing. What I'm saying here is that I didn't even grasp what malted barley smelled like until I was standing knee-deep in it. So my advice is to not look too hard for "malty." I don't use "biscuit" either, for the record. Tell someone in the United States that a whiskey has a hint of "biscuit" and he'll picture a round, puffy, and usually savory baked bread. To the person in the U.K.? A biscuit is a cookie. That's just too confusing all around. I will say this: Whiskey that has a high percentage of barley, or is made entirely of barley, tends to nose less sweet and taste drier in comparison with whiskeys that are made with our next grain workhorse, corn.

## Corn

American whiskey producers are famous for using corn in their whiskey, and that makes a lot of sense when you think about what sort of grain American pioneers found growing aplenty when they got here. Corn lends an incredible sweetness to the palate compared with other grains. If you rub your hands together with a splash of some fresh, unaged high-content corn whiskey, you'll marvel at how cornlike it actually smells. Corn aromas mellow out over time in wood, lending a more balanced sweetness to the palate.

## Rye

If you love a barrage of spices like cloves and pepper, accompanied by a mouth-puckering feel, look no further than whiskeys made with a hefty amount of rye in their mash bill. Most rye-based whiskey now comes from the United States and will aptly say "rye whiskey" right on the label. Canadians use the words "whisky" and "rye" interchangeably, even though the practice of using rye has given way to corn in most big-brand Canadian whiskies like Crown Royal. Corn is cheaper and easier to grow.

## Wheat

Wheat rounds out the top four grain players, and it typically lends a somewhat floral, delicate, or green quality to a whiskey. I haven't given you bourbon basics yet, but you'll probably see wheat most often referenced on labels that call their whiskeys "wheated bourbon." Wheat whiskeys are on the rise in America as new whiskey makers scramble to quench America's thirst for all things whiskey.

### GRAPE VERSUS GRAIN

We often call out wines by the grape varietal—chardonnay, pinot, and merlot—because the grape varietal practically defines the taste, color, and style of the wine. In fact, grapes influence the flavor of wine to a much greater degree than grain influences the flavor of a whiskey. The Scotch Whisky Association estimates that more than 70 percent of a whiskey's flavor actually comes from wood while many bourbon makers in the United States put that number closer to 50 percent.

## WHISKEY BEGINS AS BEER

All grains—malted or not—are milled into powders and husks and then soaked in scalding water to extract the sugars in a vessel called the mash tun or mash cooker. Think of the mash as hot, grainy, flavorful tea. Sugars are extracted from the grains at different water temperatures, which is why Americans call the vessel a mash cooker—grains "cook" at different temperatures.

There are two schools of thought about what should happen next. Either you leave all those solids in the liquid as you move on to the next activity (fermentation) or you don't. In Scotland, for example, distilleries filter the hot sugary liquid by draining it through a giant sieve at the bottom of the mash tun and then divert what's now called the wort into a vessel called a washback for fermentation. Americans generally leave all those solids in the liquid during fermentation (and even during distillation). The decision is a subjective one because there are no rules or mandates about how a distillery mashes.

## Fermentation

All the alcoholic beverages you enjoy require some sort of fermentation: a process by which a living organism (yeast) converts a sugar into alcohol. In wine, the yeast feeds on the sugars of the grape (monosaccharides like glucose and fructose) to create alcohol, and in whiskey they feast on all those nice sugary starches (polysaccharides). The mash is poured into large wooden or steel vats, the yeast is added, and a pretty wild-looking chemical reaction happens. As the yeast feeds off sugar, it releases carbon dioxide, which bubbles up aggressively. Once I climbed a ladder to peek over a two-story washback in Scotland and discovered big spinning blades whirling around the top to break the carbon dioxide bubbles and prevent them from spilling over the edge. That's a tremendous amount of energy when you think about it. Many of the esters that are responsible for fruity, floral, and green aromas develop at this stage (see chapter 1).

### Yeast and Whiskey Flavor

The type of yeast used will affect flavor as well. I started appreciating a yeast's effect on flavor late in the game because I'd spent so much time studying in Scotland, where distilleries, specialty whisky stores, and whisky enthusiasts explained to me that the importance of yeast is measured only by the amount of sugar it can consume—in other words, alcohol yield—rather than its flavor. In fact, a celebrated Edinburgh whisky shop writes online that yeast is "one of the less significant factors when it comes to the flavor of whisky." I'll tell you why I don't agree.

Yeasts are single-celled living fungi and are very common in nature. They can live on the skins of fruits such as peaches, apples, and berries; are found in soil, water, and on our skin; basically yeast is everywhere. American distilleries Four Roses, Heaven Hill, Maker's Mark, Wild Turkey, Jim Beam, and Early Times, and many other smaller craft distillers "mother" their yeast strains by carefully cultivating them in a special container called the dona tub in what's called, aptly, the dona room. Distillers are wildly protective about how their yeast is cultivated—some of the methods they use have been passed down for generations. Sacred secrets can include using hops or fine-tuning the temperatures in the dona tub in a particular way. I visited the Four Roses Distillery in Kentucky and sampled different whiskeys, all created under the same conditions and with the same methods except for one thing: the yeast strain. One tasted more floral, one nuttier, one more cereallike, and one more fruity. I was sold. I don't argue with my tongue and nose. Yeast can definitely influence whiskey character. Given that producers in America are successfully playing around with yeast, I predict that you will see more Scottish producers moving toward increased yeast experimentation, too.

## DISTILLATION: WAIT, WHAT IS DISTILLATION ANYWAY?

*Stay with me here.* Distillation is simply a physical separation process that occurs among molecules as a liquid is heated and then condensed back into a liquid again. The separation process is based on molecular weight. Heavier (bigger) molecules need more energy to become volatile to transition from a liquid phase to a vapor (gas) phase. As you heat a solution, the lighter molecules will volatize first. As you condense these vapors by cooling them, they will precipitate into a liquid again. That's distillation. The word derives from the Latin *de-stillaire*, or "trickle down." Distillation was probably first used to make saltwater potable, and was later used to create balms and perfumes to cover unpleasant smells for royalty or prepare the dead for burial.

With regard to whiskey, alcohol and water both evaporate at different temperatures: alcohol at 173 degrees Fahrenheit and water at 212 degrees Fahrenheit. When spirit is heated in a still, the idea is to create an aromatic-rich vapor, collect the vapor, and then condense it back into a liquid (distillate) before putting the liquid into casks for aging. There are myriad still shapes, styles, and methods a distiller can use to tweak the amount and kinds of aromatic alcohol collected. This ultimately helps contribute to the overall character of a whiskey. Wine is not distilled—in other words, it is not heated to release the aromatic molecules the way whiskey is. Distillation is a beautiful thing once you understand the basic concepts of why and how it is done.

## Early Pot Still

*Early American rudimentary pot still with coiled condenser*

The original alcohol distillation apparatus was called an alembic still, and its name comes from the Arab word *al-imbiq*. Most sources point to a Persian alchemist named Jābir ibn Hayyān as the creator of the original still circa AD 800 (should the question arise during *Jeopardy!*). Yet I prefer whiskey historian Fred Minnick's version of history, which he explains in *Whiskey Women: The Untold Story of How Women Saved Bourbon, Scotch, and Irish Whiskey.* He says that women were the first distillers; specifically they were Alexandrian Egyptian alchemists from the first through third centuries. Over coffee one afternoon in New York, Fred explained that giving women credit for creating the first stills is common sense: "Think about it," he said. "Women historically are the ones in charge of cooking and cleaning. Distillation happened in kitchens." Who can argue with that logic?

His research suggests that alchemist Maria Hebraea, or "Maria the Jewess," probably made the first still by connecting two hollow vessels with a tube. Liquid would have been heated in the first vessel to create aromatic vapors in an onion- or teardrop-shaped container, cooled, and then diverted through the tube to a second vessel, or a receiver. What's amazing about the practice of distillation Maria exercised is that it hasn't changed all that much in two thousand years. Even the basic still shape—a bulbous bottom with an arm extending from the top to collect vapors and then divert them to a second vessel—is widely used, especially by small moonshine or home distillers. Pot stills, most famously used in Scotland and found all over the world, are probably the most widely recognized and celebrated ancestors of Maria's invention, but are much bigger.

Pot stills are those pretty, copper, bulbous, long-necked stills that stretch out of a big rounded bottom. Smaller distilleries use just a few of them, large distilleries can house a dozen (or two) of them. As the fermented liquid (wort) is heated, different aromatic compounds carry a whiskey's aroma up what is called the swan neck. If the swan neck is extraordinarily long, like those on the pot stills at the Glenmorangie Distillery that stand at a whopping twenty-six feet high, only the lightest and most delicate compounds weave their way up and over. As a result, Glenmorangie noses subtly and elegantly—floral and fruity, you might say. (Perhaps you noticed that during your tasting, if you chose to use the Glenmorangie 10 to explore.) Short, squat pot stills, like those found at The Macallan Distillery, make it easier for some of the larger, heavier molecules to make their way into the condensed spirit. Because of this, the rich, nuttier, and more robust taste of The Macallan can be attributed partly to Macallan's style of still.

## Pot Still

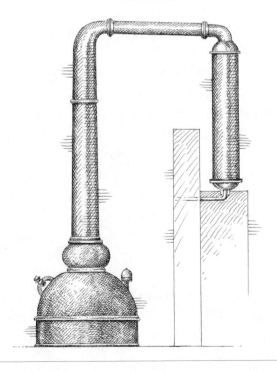

*Pot still*

Most whiskey made in pot stills is either double distilled or triple distilled. Each time a whiskey is heated, condensed, and collected, we call that a distillation. Do that twice and call it double distilled. Three times? I think you get it now. Ireland is very famous for triple distilled whiskey, although not all of its whiskeys are triple distilled. Only one distillery in Scotland, Auchentoshan, is triple distilled—another whiskey tidbit that pops up with whiskey connoisseurs at my bar. I've never heard of a quadruple distilled whiskey, in case you are wondering.

Talking about distillation gives me a great opportunity to talk to you again about the myth that older whiskeys are always better whiskeys. Many of those delicate "estery" aromas I described earlier develop during the distillation process. Whiskey makers take great pride in tweaking how they distill their spirit to maximize pleasing aromatics. The younger a whiskey, the closer it is to the clear, essential qualities of the spirit when it comes out of the pot still because the wood hasn't had as much time to silence some of the delicate aromas. I love some of the citrus, floral, pear, and apple notes that can become masked over time by the effects of wood.

Many distillers spend years learning how to coax and tweak esters from a pot still to create a perfect symphony of aroma and flavor. Whether a still is lit by fire or coils from the inside affects this process, as does how slow or fast a pot is heated. The size and shape of a still also has a dramatic impact on whiskey flavor.

## Column Stills

Column stills operate with the same goal as the pot still: to capture the aromas by heating liquid to create vapor and then condensing it again. Column stills are ubiquitous throughout American bourbon making especially and are used by massive blended whiskey operations such as Johnnie Walker and Dewar's. Here's why: They can operate continuously, twenty-four hours a day. Some column stills are downright enormous—I've seen them reach four stories high. Often, column stills are referred to as continuous stills because of their ability to work around the clock. The tremendous amount of spirit output—Johnnie Walker sells 20.1 million cases of whiskey per year—gives columns an advantage over pot stills, which work in batches. Think about this: Glenfiddich sells about 1 million cases a year and claims status as the top-selling (double pot distilled) single malt Scotch. That's only one twentieth of Johnnie Walker's distribution worldwide.

Not all column stills are this large, however. Like pot stills, they come in a range of sizes. All column stills tweak flavor and extract alcohol in the same way: Steam passes up through the bottom of the column to meet the sugary and grainy mash bill (sometimes called beer) poured from the top, while perforated metal plates lie flat along the length of the column capturing husks, seeds, and other grain remnants as the starchy liquid falls. The flavor-rich steam meets starchy goodness at all these levels as it rises to the top and condenses. The steam at the bottom is very hot and becomes cooler as it rises. Alcohol volatizes at a lower temperature; the cooler temperatures toward the top where the aromatic spirit condenses will contain more alcohol than water. For this reason, column stills are great at making a higher-proof spirit than pot stills.

An Irish taxman named Aeneas Coffey patented the column, or continuous, still. After collecting taxes from whiskey makers during his time working for the Irish government, Coffey resigned in 1824 to build his own still, which came out in 1830. I call that a whiskey atonement. Scotland was quick to pick up this efficient whiskey-making technology. Some credit Scotland's adoption of the Coffey still and Ireland's ironic refusal to use it (because it wasn't considered as authentic, even though an Irishman invented it) as one of the factors in why Irish whiskey struggled and Scottish whisky flourished in the late nineteenth century.

## Hybrid Stills

*Hybrid still*

Many new distilleries built in the U.S.A. use hybrid still equipment—a combination of a pot still and a column still. Should you visit a small distillery, you'll probably see a hybrid in use. It allows distilleries flexibility because gin, vodka, and brandy can be distilled in the column as well as whiskey.

## HEADS, HEARTS, AND TAILS

Distillers watch the distillate pouring out of the still, which comes out in phases nicknamed heads, hearts, and tails. The first distillate out of the run, called the head, carries many unwanted notes, as does what they call the tail, or the end of the run. Where the distiller makes the cut to capture the "heart" is an art. The heart of the run is what is put into casking for maturation, and should carry all the balanced and desired flavors that were created during mashing, fermentation, and distillation.

# MATURATION: WOOD HAS FLAVOR!

The time whiskey spends in a cask is called maturation. In other words, maturation is the time that the spirit spends aging, gaining complexity, and picking up aromatic layers along the way. But not all wood is created equal. And distillers have many choices when it comes to this step in the process. Different casks create different flavors, and combinations of casks can even be vatted together (that is, mixed or intermingled) to create your favorite brand of whiskey. *Vatting casks together does not make a whiskey a blend. Vatting casks together does not make a whiskey a blend.* No, that's not a typo. It's one of the most confusing concepts for newcomers to grasp so I'm telling you twice. Even seasoned whiskey aficionados still become confused when we talk about how whiskey makers can take advantage of all the casks sitting in their warehouses and mix them together (or not) to create flavor. But what we call a blended whiskey is an entirely different concept, and one I'll explain more in chapter 3.

To make things more complicated, some whiskeys age in several different types of casks before they are bottled as part of their maturation. For example, Auchentoshan Three Wood (master blender Rachel Barrie) is matured in refill bourbon, ex–Spanish oloroso sherry butts, and ex–Pedro Ximenez butts. Spirit literally moves from one cask into another over a period of time to create the flavors, then it is finally vatted together with other whiskeys that followed the same process to create one big batch for a bottling.

Wood might very well win the award for flavor contribution in your dram. We talked about many of those woody aromas in chapter 1: leather, oak, vanilla, fig, and spice are a few. The Scotch Whisky Association in Scotland states that close to 70 percent of the flavor of a whiskey actually comes from the cask wood. Distiller Chris Morris from U.S. whiskey giant Brown-Forman claims that number is closer to 50 percent. Either way, it's significant. I don't mean that other whiskey-making steps aren't important—distillers who meticulously monitor the process every inch of the way make the best whiskeys. There is real skill involved. But you can really mess up your whiskey if something goes wrong during maturation. For example, leave a whiskey in too long and it will taste too bitter. It might taste as if you were biting into your toothpick. Take the whiskey out of the wood too soon and it won't develop to its full potential.

Oak used for aging whiskey comes loaded with flavor all bound up in the tiny cell walls, membranes, openings, and intricate layers within the wood. It's literally *loaded* with flavor. New-make spirit—the stuff that comes right out of the still—seeps into all those wood nooks and crannies, intermingling with wood starches (which you know now are essentially sugars). Some wood compounds break down when spirit is added, some new aromatic molecules are created out of the interaction between wood and spirit, and a little of what some distillers call magic happens, all contributing to those wonderful aromatics that fall under the "woody" heading. One of wood's compounds, called lignin, is responsible for most of the aromatics released into your whiskey: vanilla, spice, peach, and coconut. Tannic acids, which create those mouth-puckery, drying feelings that both whiskey and wine lovers look for in balance, are also released by wood.

## Tie a Yellow Ribbon 'Round That Old Whiskey Tree

Port Pipe

Gorda

Bourbon

Puncheon

Hogshead

Butt

Blood Tub

ASB

Quarter Cask

*Not all casks are created equal. Barrels, butts, hogsheads, and quarter casks are the most popular sizes used by whiskey makers around the world.*

Two oak species are used for whiskey maturation and can also determine whiskey character: American white oak, *Quercus alba*, or European oak, *Quercus robur*. Each wood species delivers a different cast of flavors, or the same flavors but to different degrees.

To make a cask, an oak tree is sliced into long wooden staves, bent through a heating process, and held together with metal hoops. Cask heads will be hammered into each end and sealed with reeds so that no liquid leaks. Into the belly of a cask a hole is punched for filling and emptying liquid. A wooden plug called the bung seals the hole. The term "cask" is actually another umbrella term: Barrels and butts are the two most popular types of casks used worldwide. A barrel contains 53 gallons of spirit (approximately 267 bottles of whiskey), not including some of the evaporation that might occur. A butt, the type of cask that holds Spanish sherry, is gigantic: These casks can hold a whopping 132 gallons of whiskey, more than double a barrel's amount.

### American Casks Versus Casks Around the World

American whiskey must by law mature in fresh "virgin oak" barrels. Scotland, Japan, and Ireland do not have that regulation, and often mature their whiskeys in refill casks—casks that used to hold bourbon—or Spanish sherry butts that once aged sherry (more on sherry casks in the next section). Bourbon casks and most refill casks are made from American oak.

Stacked rows of casks inscribed with painted lids that read "Jim Beam" dot the Scottish landscape, waiting to be refurbished and repainted for maturation. The sight surprised me the first time I saw the casks on the Isle of Arran off the west coast of Scotland, so far away from Kentucky. But refill casks are a better option for aging Scotch, Irish whiskeys, and Japanese whiskies because new oak can overpower the subtle flavors of barley spirit.

American whiskey, much of it made using corn and rye, can handle the big rush of flavors that come quickly and strongly out of new wood: vanilla, coconuts, spice, and tannins to name a few. New wood is also what gives American whiskey the big and bold character that people love. Imagine taking a new tea bag and steeping it in your water; you need only a couple of minutes to get all that flavor into your liquid. Every time you reuse it, you'd have to steep it longer to get flavor, and that flavor would be subtler. Think of new wood the same way. American whiskeys are the first dunk of a tea bag.

Many non–American whiskey distillers now vat some virgin oak casks into a few of the whiskey brands they sell because it adds a nice flavor to a distiller's "cask recipe," as I like to call it. Scotch, Irish, and Japanese whiskeys that use virgin oak barrels will usually say so right on the label. For the most part, however, expect that your non-American whiskey will have had much of its contents sitting in seasoned and mellowed "refill bourbon barrels." You'll start seeing the phrase "refill bourbon barrel" or "second-fill bourbon barrel" as you start observing whiskey labels from around the world. A distiller can keep reusing barrels as long as they contribute flavor, but personally I haven't ever seen any fourth- or fifth-fill barrels being used by any whiskey brands I like.

### Scotch and Sherry Casks

Sherry—a fortified wine from Spain—provided Scotland with the original "recycled" casks. Sherry butts aren't easy to pluck from Spain, though; not only do sherry producers use their perfectly seasoned wine butts until they disintegrate or rot sets in, but because very few people partake in an evening glass of sherry anymore (I expect a resurgence), there isn't much sherry being produced these days. To skirt the problem, Scotch whisky makers commission historic sherry bodegas like González Byass to build and season sherry butts by the thousands using American oak. Yes, that's right, American oak. This might surprise some of you who assume that when whiskey matures in ex-sherry casks, it also means that the cask wood was created out of European oak. I've even seen experts, bloggers, reviewers, magazine articles, and mixologists equate a sherry-influenced cask with European oak. But sherry can be filled in either type of cask.

Whiskey makers *sort of* tell you about the wood used for aging whiskey in ex-sherry casks. As in, they'll tell you what kind of sherry was used, but they won't say whether the wood is European oak or American oak. I'm not sure why whiskey makers don't make that clear on the bottle. Either they don't think it's important for you to know the type of oak used, or they'd rather you think it's made from European oak, which some whiskey drinkers think is superior (not necessarily so). Very broadly, American oak delivers more coconut and vanilla flavors while European oak is subtler, delivering spice, pruney, or fig notes. The Macallan is the most popular whiskey on the market that uses true European oak. How will you know? On the label, look for Aged in Ex-Oloroso casks or Aged in Ex–Pedro Ximenez casks, or a combination of both. Those are the two types of sherry you'll see most often listed on the label. Notice they won't say European oak, though. If true European oak casks are used, the bottle will probably say so—at least I think it should.

Sherry producers actually began importing American oak at least *two centuries* ago. A botanist named Esteban Boutelou wrote in 1807: "The great wine shippers . . . use oak almost exclusively, and they esteem more than any that which comes from the United States of America."

Sherry-influenced whiskeys are often described as sweet because sherry is a sweet wine. But this is misleading. Whiskeys that use a high ratio of ex-sherry casks for aging actually taste drier and nuttier than whiskeys aged in old bourbon barrels. Describing sherry-cask-aged whiskey as sweet is held over from the British perspective on sherry. There are more sherry drinkers in the U.K. and it is indeed sweeter than nonfortified wines. But, really, bourbon casks impart sweeter-associated aromatics than sherry casks do. Most whiskey drinkers—Americans, especially—will think whiskey aged in sherry tastes drier than those aged in bourbon casks. Think stewed raisins and figs versus coconut birthday cake.

## Charring Versus Toasting

Bourbon barrels are burned on the inside with a live flame to prep the casks for spirits. Charring a cask creates a warm and sugary coating that helps pull flavors like vanilla out of the wood. The resulting charcoal layer also serves as a filter, keeping unsavory notes like sulfur out of your spirit. Char levels, from one to four, are determined by the thickness of the char and executed by the length of time the wood is exposed to the flames. Most American whiskey barrels are charred to level three or four. You'll get good at detecting the pleasant but subtle effect of charred wood on your spirit—it's almost like the smell of fresh pencil shavings with a hint of sweet smoke. Refill barrels are recharred in places like Scotland, Ireland, and Japan. I'm often asked if a particular Scotch, then, can take on some characteristics of a whiskey like Jim Beam. The idea is to get at those nice caramels and sugars, not the taste of the whiskey itself, so, no—your Scotch will not taste at all like Jim Beam when Beam's barrels are refilled in Scotland.

Some casks are toasted—toasting exposes wood to high heat without exposing the surface to an actual flame. Many of the same compounds seep into a toasted cask, with the exception of those compounds that are added by the char (called additive flavors) or subtracted by the char (called subtractive flavors). How long a cask is toasted or charred, how deeply into the wood the burned layer penetrates, and the type of wood used are some of the details a whiskey maker considers.

## Wood "Finishing"

Once a whiskey meets the aging requirements set by the mother country's regulations, a whiskey maker might decide to finish a whiskey in an old rum cask, a port cask (called a pipe), a Madeira or even a Sauternes wine cask—whatever the whiskey producer feels will enhance or complement the whiskey produced at his or her distillery. The word "finish" here refers to the extra maturation time in a uniquely seasoned cask before it's bottled. The label will usually describe the particular details of the finishing as well as the original casks used for the maturation.

## Japanese Casks

Mizunara casks—Japanese oak—lend a sandalwood and a slight floral aromatic to some Japanese whiskies. I've started seeing Mizunara referenced on some Scotch bottles as of late, and wouldn't be surprised if by the time this book comes out there will be a few more.

## Other Casks You Might See Listed on Your Label

We haven't exhausted our wood conversation quite yet. I could write an entire other book just about wood! But I do want you to be familiar with all the lingo. Small distilleries in the United States and new distilleries popping up in regions like Sweden or Tasmania use small casks called quarter casks. These little guys (a quarter of the size of a traditional barrel) will age the spirit quickly because of the high ratio of spirit to wood contact, and help a distillery get some nice aged whiskey out the door without having to wait too long. Other casks, called hogsheads, puncheons, and gordas, will also populate a distillery's warehouse—especially in Scotland, Ireland, and Japan, although they are not nearly as prevalent. Just be aware that they're bench players out there and that they can be part of a mix if a distiller wants them to be.

## WHISKEY-MAKING BASICS

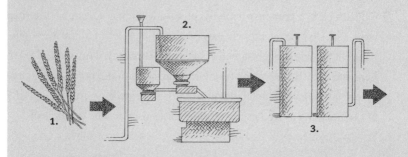

### 1. GRAIN

The four most common grains used are corn, barley, rye, and wheat.

### 2. MILLING

The dried barley, corn, rye, or other grains are ground into a starchy powder. Mashing grains are dumped into vats and soaked in warm water, sort of like a giant vat of tea, to release sugars.

### 3. FERMENTATION

Yeast is added to the mash and feeds of the sugars, releasing $CO_2$ and creating alcohol.

### 4. DISTILLATION

Distillation is the process of heating that fermented liquid to

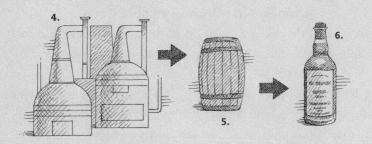

create vapors and then condensing those vapors back to liq-uids. Depending on the distillery, different kinds of stills are used.

## 5. MATURATION
Freshly distilled spirit is put into different casks and then moved to a warehouse for aging. "Maturation" is the word used to describe the period of time the whiskey sleeps in the casks, absorbing all the flavor and environmental (if any) in-fluences.

## 6. BOTTLING
Producers release their whiskeys in many different types of "bottlings," such as single barrel, single cask, cask strength, non–chill filtered, and small batch.

## FROM CASK TO BOTTLE

### Please Don't Skim This Section! I Will Help You Unlock That Whiskey Label Code

A member of the distillery team called the master blender is tasked with the job of deciding how to put casks together to create a particular bottle of whiskey. What they decide to do will often be reflected on the label. Terms like "single barrel," "single cask," "cask strength," "non–chill filtered," and "small batch" are all part of a master blender's process and influence (and are sometimes a reflection of a marketing team that wants a master blender to make whiskey based on an idea of what it thinks the public wants). I know this can be very confusing, as we are *still* not talking about blended whiskey. We are talking about how the contents of different casks come together to become one whiskey.

### Vatting

Most whiskey is vatted, or batched. That means that the master blender chooses a bunch of casks to mingle before bottling. If a smaller number of casks are vatted (batched) together than what is normally batched at the distillery, it is called a small batch. In America, a master blender will choose to vat a set of various virgin oak casks, all of which deliver subtleties in flavor. In other whiskey-producing regions, the choices can include a dizzying number of options of casks to vat: whiskey that's been aged in virgin oak barrels, ex-sherry butts, used bourbon barrels, Mizunara casks, wine casks—you name it, and in all sorts of proportions, too.

In addition, the same whiskey can mature in different casks before it's vatted. They can simply be aged in one cask and then dumped together with others right before bottling a batch.

## SMALL BATCH

**Small batch** is largely an American term. It's used when a smaller number of casks than usual are mingled together to create a special expression from a distiller. For example, Four Roses Small Batch versus its more widely produced Four Roses Yellow Label. New, smaller craft distilleries always produce small batch whiskeys because they don't have any other choice—everything they do is small, which makes the whole term rather fluid and confusing, if you ask me. But you'll see the term on bottles nonetheless.

## NOTES FROM A MASTER BLENDER

My role as a master blender of a distillery is to mix different casks together to create a particular flavor profile, and then bottle it. Every Friday night, I sit at a long wooden table with a bunch of samples in front of me from various casks and taste them. I'll take notes and then decide which barrels to mix together, how many, and in which proportions they should be mixed. It reminds me of making mud pies like I did as a kid, but with whiskey.

Batching is probably the most fun part of my job—but there is a lot more to it. I also need to know the barrels that I am in charge of and the whiskey inside them: How many barrels do I have? How old are they? What are they like, on average? Are there particular notes that show up more often than others? How do the flavors and aromas tend to change over time? Are the barrels on the sunny side of the room different from the ones on the shady side? Did we have any production hiccups that might affect the quality of the whiskey? When did we get that great batch of corn? Where are those barrels?

Even if I have a good understanding of each individual barrel's contents, it won't get me all the way to beautiful whiskey. I also predict what will happen when those barrels mix together: Which aromas will be highlighted and which will be diluted? Will that beautiful, herbaceous smell from barrel (sample) number 265 lend a pleasant note to the final product or make it smell like dish soap? Also, what should the bourbon taste like? How does my spirit compare with others on the market? Will anybody besides me enjoy what I'm creating?

I suspect that even the best blenders don't always know the answers to all (or even most) of those questions—the nature of maturing whiskey is somewhat unpredictable. I've put in a lot of time and I've trained with whiskey makers who possess more knowledge than I. I've learned to recognize commonalities and trends and come to understand my whiskey, much in the way that I imagine a painter understands color and light and canvas.

—Nicole Austin, Master Blender, King's County Distillery, Brooklyn, New York

## Single Barrel/Single Cask

Whiskey dumped from one barrel or cask into bottles is called—you guessed it—single barrel or single cask. Blanton's Original Single Barrel, Evan Williams Single Barrel, and The Balvenie Single Barrel are examples of this style. And because Blanton's and Evan Williams are American whiskeys, you know now exactly what kind of cask was used (hint: 100 percent charred virgin oak).

## Dilution and Cask Strength

Most whiskey is diluted with a bit of water before bottling to bring the alcohol strength down to around 40 percent, or to a place the master distiller thinks tastes best for his or her whiskey. When I see a bottle with a very high alcohol by volume listed—above 50 percent or so—that's my clue that a whiskey has not been diluted with spring water first, in which case the label will probably call it cask strength.

### INDEPENDENT BOTTLING

A distiller can also decide to sell its casks to an independent bottler or blended whiskey maker to resell the whiskey under different brand names. Gordon & MacPhail in Scotland is an example of an independent bottler; Compass Box is a boutique Scotch blend company. They tell you so right on their labels. In America, however, both distillate and aged whiskey can be sold to independent companies as it is in Scotland, but we do not have a name for this practice nor is it very easy to tell which whiskey is actually bought or sourced from another producer. Distilleries that sell their casks or distillate usually remain quiet about it. I get into that in the American whiskey section in chapter 3.

## Chill Filtration

One process many whiskeys undergo before bottling is called chill filtration. I know this sounds technical and it is, but you will come across bottles that refer to this practice, and I want to make sure you know exactly what it means. Chill filtration is a process by which the whiskey is chilled (cooled) before bottling so that fatty acids, lipids, and any other wood sediment can be separated from the liquid and taken out. Picture salad dressing in your refrigerator—the oils separate from the other liquids and spices. Once the insoluble parts of a whiskey separate post chilling, the whiskey is put through a filter or chill filtration machine. Non–chill filtered whiskeys offer a richer and thicker texture, with fatty acids swimming around in the dram. Some say they offer more flavor and are a higher quality, but I think that all depends on the distiller and the particular whiskey. I don't like making a sweeping rule like that. Also, a whiskey company can chill filter the whiskey in different ways at different temperatures, separating out various sizes of those fatty acids, playing with texture, mouthfeel, and ultimately the beauty of the spirit.

Non–chill filtered whiskeys become cloudy when water is added; I've also seen sediment floating in a non–chill filtered whiskey—two reasons why distillers choose to chill filter. They'd rather avoid consumer complaints of "cloudy and dirty whiskey." Also, non–chill filtered whiskeys are mostly bottled at cask strength and therefore contain a higher ABV. I've sipped non–chill filtered, cask strength whiskey at 70 percent ABV. It is perfectly acceptable, if not expected, to add water to a whiskey like that to mellow the whiskey a little bit, or as whiskey insiders say, to bring down the heat.

The choices a master blender makes between casking and bottling seem endless. Read the labels to get as much info about the bottle as you can. As we go into deeper detail in the following chapter, I'll fill in the gaps. Failing that, I get online and do a bit of research to see what went into the bottle I'm drinking.

Unraveling Bottle Lingo: Double Versus Single—the Rundown: I'm going to SINGLE out the word "SINGLE" because this SINGLE word can be confusing. And Double that.

**Single Barrel or Single Cask Whiskey:** Whiskey that has been aged and bottled out of one single barrel or cask. Blanton's Original Single Barrel is one of the well-known American single barrel whiskeys, and The Balvenie 15-Year Single Barrel is a more widely popular single malt Scotch single cask offering. If a whiskey is not designated as single barrel or single cask, it has been batched over a set of selected casks. Most whiskeys are batched rather than sold as single barrel or single cask whiskeys.

**Single Malt Scotch:** The "single" in single malt Scotch refers to one single distillery, and "malt" describes a style of whiskey in Scotland. Lagavulin, Laphroaig, Glenmorangie, and Auchentoshan are all distilleries producing single malt Scotch.

**Single Grain Whiskey:** In Scotland, "single" refers to the single distillery making grain whisky. It does not refer to one single type of grain used.

**Single Malt:** If the word "Scotch" isn't attached, it's a whiskey made outside of Scotland and using mostly or all malted barley for its starch source.

**Double Black:** This is a marketing term used to describe a style of an "extra peated" whiskey in the Johnnie Walker Black range. It is not a term used industrywide to describe whiskeys.

**Double Matured:** This is a maturing method that describes pulling the entire contents out of one cask and placing it into another. The Balvenie DoubleWood is double matured. After eleven years in one bourbon barrel, the contents are emptied into a large sherry butt for additional maturation of about one year.

**Double Barrel:** A very confusing term, used mostly for marketing purposes to make special bottlings stand out. I've seen this tag on a bottle that had two different distilleries represented within the bottle (as in a Highland Park/Bowmore Double Barrel). But that's essentially a blended malt Scotch. I've also seen Applebee's advertise "Sizzling Double Barrel Whisky Sirloins." I couldn't possibly tell you what that means, but the ad is set to a Run DMC song ("It's Tricky") and has footage of a flashy "flair" bartender who flips bottles, utensils, and ingredients. Double the fun, I guess.

## BEYOND WOOD: OTHER FACTORS CAN CHANGE A WHISKEY'S PERSONALITY

### Terroir = Flavor Making!

I moved to Scotland during a seasonally balmy autumn in 2005, and by Christmas I was still wearing only my leather jacket, leaving that North Face puffer jacket silliness I used to rely on at home in New York City behind. "Isn't this nice?" I would think to myself as the sun barely rose above the horizon by noon, casting a haunting and beautiful sideways light before setting again at four. But by July that same year I was still wearing that damned leather jacket, with British coins and lipsticks jingling in the hem after they'd squeezed through worn pocket holes. I stomped around in mud-soaked motorcycle boots, blowing my nose and firing up the gas fireplace by night, all while cursing the Scottish summer. I remember once sitting in a café on the remote and treeless island of Orkney, trying to warm up on the Fourth of July. I'd been sent to northern Scotland every summer for five years running as an ambassador for Glenfiddich and I was feeling a little bit bitter—most of my friends at home were on the beach. I tried to remain positive, reframing my outlook, willing the dreary day to turn into a romantic and wistful one. I reached over my milky black tea for the stack of damp and ratty café magazines and noticed that the top rag featured an Italian Riviera article. The model on the cover was wearing a tiny summer dress and heels, her arms cupped around a dude's waist while they rode on the back of a Vespa. The Mediterranean sparkled in the distance. "You should be here," the title read. "Yes, yes, I should be there!" I cried while shoving the last crumbs of a scone into my mouth. This unforgiving climate is precisely what helps make whisky creation so awesome in Scotland.

Later that day I fell in love with Scapa 16.

Climate, soil, sun, weather, and vineyard location all claim tremendous credit for the health and life of a grape vine and the wine's taste. Many whiskey enthusiasts champion the terroir concept, too, although arguing that these earthly elements wield that same power over whiskey's flavor that they do over wine is debatable.

I believe that terroir contributes to flavor in whiskey, to a certain extent. But whiskey making, as you now know, also lies in the hands of a skilled distillery team that performs a mix of skill and magic during the process from grain to bottle. Big brands in Scotland love to tell dramatic stories of the sea and wind lapping against their warehouses, throwing spray filled with salt and mist into the atmosphere and contributing to the briny or salty taste sometimes found in single malt Scotches. You'll hear about fresh burns (streams) and glens (valleys) weaving through distillery grounds, casting mystery upon the spirit in barrels. In America, the image of fresh, clean, iron-free limestone water rich in calcium being poured into whiskey bottles to produce the highest quality bourbons is ubiquitous. I fall for these images and stories every time. But, where does fact meet fiction? Where do elements of terroir affect our whiskey taste?

### Climate

Kentucky gets darn hot and humid in July, leaving you gasping for a mint julep and air-conditioning. By January, it's cold enough to ice-skate. In response to temperature changes, cask wood expands and contracts, absorbing more whiskey in the heat and closing up shop to rest for a time during the winter slumber. Distillers say that the casks "breathe" throughout the seasons, contributing to the character of your favorite Kentucky brands like Buffalo Trace, Marker's Mark, and Wild Turkey. I once visited Wild Turkey's warehouses and rubbed my hand along a warped cask head, which reminded me of old vinyl records distorted from the sun and being unable to fix the needle into a groove. "That's because of the temperature changes here," master distiller Jimmy Russell explained to me. "Happens all the time." I had never witnessed warped cask heads in Scotland, where temperatures don't fluctuate so drastically. The Gulf Stream keeps it nice and temperate in the Celtic countries.

Very simply, climate changes the speed at which a whiskey ages as well as the whiskey's evaporation rates, both of which will affect a whiskey's palate. Heat encourages water to evaporate and seep through the casks—high heat draws out the water. Because alcohol doesn't penetrate through wood the way water does, the alcohol proof inside a cask can increase because of water loss. The never-too-cold, never-too-hot warehouses in places like Scotland keep whiskey evaporation rates at about 3 percent per year, an amount they call the "angel's share," while Kentucky warehouses can see an 8 percent whiskey loss in a year, something I call the "drunken angel's share." New whiskey distilleries in places like upstate New York and Texas play with temperature-controlled warehouses to shelter casks from extreme heat or cold and to experiment with the effects of climate on flavor. Japanese and other whiskeys around the world must manage temperature implications on spirit, with many regions developing systems like climate-controlled warehouses or shipping of casks to places where the environment is less volatile for aging.

Even microclimates within warehouses can mess with evaporation rates of the spirit, depending on whether the cask is stacked atop ten others or whether it kisses a dirt floor. The temperature variance between the bottom of a warehouse and the top of a warehouse in Kentucky can be as much as forty degrees. Maker's Mark Distillery places freshly filled barrels in the upper half of the warehouse for the first three years of maturation, and after that time the spirit is moved to the bottom half for the rest.

The effects of temperature on whiskeys from major whiskey-producing regions with different climates versus the effects of temperature on different casks within one region such as Scotland are harder to explore, and up for debate. If we were to keep whiskey-making methods the same—grain, pot still size, maturation, water, etc.—and make one whiskey in Kentucky and the other in northern Scotland, you'd probably find a big difference in flavor. The Kentucky whiskey, because it's exposed to wide fluctuations in temperature, ages more quickly. The heat expands the wood, allowing the spirit to seep into its pores more easily. Do the same experiment, this time produce them both in Scotland—one in the north and one in the south—you'd probably arrive at whiskeys tasting more similar. As far as I know, no one's swapped whiskey for aging between the United States and Ireland or Scotland. If they did, the results are top secret, I guess.

### "It's All About Proof and Aging"

Because heat encourages water evaporation and leaves behind a higher-proof alcoholic spirit, the timing of when a whiskey is removed from a cask is very important. A distillery wants to empty a cask at that magic moment before it turns into something woody and undrinkable. Distillers will also pay close attention to the percentage of alcohol in the spirit going *into* the cask before aging. They know that as the water evaporates, alcohol percentage rises, and therefore some water might be required to bring that heat down before bottling it. When you see "cask strength" or "barrel proof" on the label, this is your promise from the distillery that no water was added to the whiskey before bottling.

Ideally, the lower the alcohol percentage of a spirit coming off a still into cask, the less water will be needed after maturation to bring the heat down to around 40 percent. Less water means more of that wood flavor. Bernie Lubbers, a brand ambassador at Kentucky's Heaven Hill, once said to me over an old-fashioned in Louisville, "Heather, it's all about proof and aging here. That's all you need to know."

### Water

I used to think that water's influence on whiskey aroma and flavor was minimal, that after the effects of distillation and after all those years maturing in a cask, the type of water used during the whiskey-making process didn't matter. So much so that I declared publicly in 2009, while sitting on a Scotch panel at a whiskey conference in New York City, that all this "water talk" was silly. Oops. I take it back. I've completely changed my mind on that.

It is still hard for me to argue that the water influence matters that much among distilleries operating in a space the size of Louisiana, or more specifically, the Highlands of Scotland. But here's some hard-core evidence that water really affects whiskey: Japanese whiskey distillers conducted some water-whiskey studies about ten years ago to uncover

Without grain, we don't have whiskey. Here is a smattering of a typical American distillery's lifeblood from the Buffalo Trace Distillery in Kentucky: corn, rye, wheat, and barley.

Floral and fruity notes bloom during distillation.

The interaction between spirit and flavor creates lustrous notes such as caramel, brown sugars, toffee, dark fruits, and vanilla.

Serve whiskey with meats, which coat your mouth and soften the reception of alcohol on our tongues.

Sink your teeth into a last winter meal of tender braised meats, potatoes, and vegetables, and pour yourself a glass of creamy Irish whiskey with notes of spring: grass, fruits, and a hint of florals.

Scotch served with a tray of charcuterie and cheeses is a memorable and easy way to entertain guests.

When all else fails, abide the adage "What grows together, goes together." Serve raw fish and Asian-inspired foods with Japanese whiskies or nonpeated single malt Scotch whiskies, after which many Japanese whiskies are modeled.

Chocolate and whiskey almost always work together, no matter what the whiskey or the chocolate.

Look for what chefs call echoed ingredients when pairing whiskey with food. Bourbon, bursting with vanillas and spice, echoes ingredients in homemade American pies like pecan, sweet potato, and pumpkin.

whether or not water really does influence flavor in a whiskey. Two distilleries owned by a company called Suntory, both of which sit on ample fresh water supplies, traded their water sources. They then made whiskey as usual, keeping everything else in the process the same: mashing, fermentation, and distillation. Mike Miyamoto, master distiller for Suntory, explained to me that the water switch not only resulted in an aromatic and taste change, but more interestingly, each distillery started expressing the taste and aroma characteristics of the other.

As it turns out, most of the great whiskeys of the world are made with what we call "soft water" sources, or water that doesn't carry high levels of magnesium and calcium. "Hard water" can become soft if minerals are removed. And here's what's interesting: You can change hard water to soft water by treating it with lime. Kentucky just so happens to sit on a limestone shelf—perhaps a good reason why water there makes for good spirit. I believe now that something in that Kentucky limestone water turns thousands of colts into magnificent racehorses and encouraged generations of distilleries to flourish in that area. There's mystery and maybe even some fact in that story. Japan and Scotland are also countries with an abundance of natural soft water sources.

**If you want to test your palate with water:**

Taste a few bottled waters like Evian, Volvic, and Contrex. Each of these waters contains different levels of mineral content. Some are saltier, some have more metallic flavors. I think it's a pretty cool graphic, and it helped convert me to the idea that water affects whiskey flavor. Suntory regularly explores the qualities different waters impart into whiskey and uses that information to refine their spirit.

## TABLE 2: HARD WATER VERSUS SOFT WATER

Soft water sources provided early whiskey makers the ability to become major whiskey producers, and indeed many of the great whiskey-producing regions of the world sit on an abundance of natural soft water sources. Water hardness is measured in ppm, referring to the parts per million of certain minerals and salts in the water. It stands to reason that the softer the water (fewer ppm), the better the water tastes. Different bottled water brands have different mineral contents. If you like a bit of water in your whiskey, and want to get really geeky about it, add soft water.

| | SOFT WATER 0–60 PPM | SEMISOFT WATER 61–120 PPM | HARD WATER 121–180 PPM | VERY HARD 181–250 PPM |
|---|---|---|---|---|
| Kentucky Distilleries | | X | | |
| Tennessee Distilleries | | X | | |
| Scottish Distilleries | | X | | |
| Japanese Distilleries | X | X | | |
| Northern Ireland Distilleries | X | | | |
| Southern Ireland Distilleries | | | X | |
| Volvic | X | | | |
| Evian | | | X | |
| Valverde | | | X | |
| Vittel | | | X | |
| Contrex | | | | X |
| Aquafina | X | | | |
| Dasani | X | | | |

Source: U.S. Geological Society and Suntory. The chart represents average hardness levels.

# 3

## Whiskey Around the World

*Scotch, American, Irish, Japanese, Canadian,
and Rest of the World Whiskeys*

_____

A story should have a beginning, a middle, and an end,
but not necessarily in that order.
JEAN-LUC GODARD

IF A WHISKEY STORY has a beginning, middle, and end, we are now
squarely in the middle. And with all due respect to Jean-Luc Godard
and French New Wave cinema directors who toy with story flow, setting
the foundation as we did in chapter 1 and in chapter 2 taking you
through the general whiskey-making process and the choices distillers
make are necessary stops on the whiskey train before we disembark here
on subregions such as Scotch and American whiskeys. If you start with
a sneak peek right into whiskey through a Scotch-only or bourbon-only
lens without placing the spirit in a bigger context of whiskey worldwide,
you are starting in the middle.

I implicate myself here—I did that, too. I used to dig right into
Scotch and talk about the use of "used casks." But "used casks" means
nothing unless you also talk about American whiskey's use of new wood
in the first place. I'd talk about the great aromas in a dram—but I didn't
stop to tell anyone at the time what "aroma" means.

I'm really happy that you made it this far. You know a heck of a lot
about whiskey—more than most know. You could even drop this book

now and go pick up that bourbon-only book or Scotch-focused book and get way more out of it than you would have before. But I hope you don't. I still have more to tell you, in my own words, about individual styles, starting with my first love, Scotch.

## SCOTCH WHISKY

*Notice how many distilleries congregate around the region called Speyside in Scotland.*

Like most things of great beauty, it is not entirely gentle and not
merely pretty, in any way . . .
MICHAEL CUNNINGHAM, *LAND'S END*

SCOTLAND IS THE BEATING heart of whisky worldwide. About 105
distilleries operate in Scotland—you'll see them wedged between rocks
and the sea or perched along the slope of a fertile hill. Scotland at its
romantic best offers a heather-laden moonscape dotted with castles and
webbed with streams, perfect for contemplating a song or a poem during
a hike. At its worst, Scotland is mud and mist for months at a time. It's
finding your car wheel stuck deeply into the earth on a crofter's property
and hoping that his walking stick cum weapon, sharpened on one side
to a dangerous point, isn't meant for your head (it was). But, hey, tough
characters and a rambling landscape create such fertile ground for
whisky, so I embrace the wild beauty of it. Approach your Scotch with
the same vigor; fall in love with flavor profiles such as brine, salt, sea,
oysters, flowers, fruit, sulfur, and smoke.

Ian Millar, global ambassador at William Grant & Sons and a
forty-year whisky-making veteran, taught me most of what I know about
Scotch whisky over the course of five years I worked with him. More
than that, I began to see that for people like Ian, whisky isn't as much of
a career as it is a way of life—a craft passed down from generations and
spread deeply into communities.

Ian is tough and bold, too. On a cold Fourth of July in 2010, we stood
on the windy edge of a prehistoric stone settlement called Skara Brae,
which was inhabited for about six hundred years between 3200 BC and
2200 BC on the isle of Orkney. Thousands of miles away in Mesopotamia
at that same time, some say, Babylonians may have invented distillation by
creating perfumes out of ethanol. I wore a down jacket. He wore a T-shirt.
Later that night, Ian bought everyone in the local pub an Orcadian
whisky—Scapa—and explained to me how pot-still size affects flavor. A
young guy mumbled incoherently and fell off the stool next to him. Ian

didn't miss a beat talking to me. "Ach, cannae worry bout im. Ee's avin a good night." Or something like that. We sipped our Scapa, and I silently predicted that for the rest of my life whenever I drank it, I would also think of lost cities, wind, and the respect we should carry for whiskey.

## Scotch Styles

Scotland produces *malt* whisky and *grain* whisky:

Malt whisky in Scotland is defined as whisky made with 100 percent malted barley.

Grain whisky in Scotland may include barley, but can involve other cereals such as corn, wheat, or rye.

In order to be called Scotch, the malt- or grain-based whiskies (or a combination of both) must be matured on Scottish soil in oak casks for a minimum of three years and bottled at a minimum of 40 percent ABV.

Five different categories of Scotch arise out of malt whisky and grain whisky production. The two styles I've highlighted below—single malt Scotch and blended Scotch whisky—make up 99.9 percent of what you will see on bar shelves.

**THE PLAYERS ARE:**

1. Single Malt Scotch
2. Blended Scotch
3. Single Grain Scotch Whisky
4. Blended Malt Scotch Whisky
5. Blended Grain Scotch Whisky

## Let's Start with the Whisky Regions

Just like France has wine regions, Scotland has distinct whisky-making regions. Historically, these regions would have clued you in as to what sort of flavor to anticipate from your bottle, but because distillers can now produce just about any flavor or style they feel like making, defining whisky flavor solely based on these designated regions makes little sense. Still, these regions are deeply part of the Scotch lexicon, which means you'll read and hear about the following five main whisky-producing areas: Highlands, Speyside, Lowlands, Campbeltown, and Islay. Single malt Scotches will list the region right on the bottle, so it's important to know a little bit about each of them, at the very least.

### Highlands

The Highlands represent the largest area of the Scotch whisky regions in Scotland, with about thirty different distilleries operating within it. Crisscrossed by single-lane roads that rise, fall, and twist around lochs and burns, the Highlands fulfill your picture-book fantasy of Caledonia. It doesn't look that different from the way it did back in the sixth century, when Irish monks penetrated the hills, looking to convert pagan farmers living in small communities—the Picts as they are now called—to Christianity. Legend says those monks brought with them distilling techniques to use in the guise of "medicinal purposes." I like to imagine that those Celtic polytheists enjoyed their first buzz as they leisurely listened to Druid monks lecture about one god. I might have swapped religions for whisky, too.

Scholars don't agree on an exact date that distillation was brought to Europe; some sources claim it came to Ireland as early as the fifth century whereas others write that it wasn't until the twelfth century. Either way, somewhere along the line the Picts went from having a bunch of gods and no booze to one god and lots of booze. Many small farms, surrounded by an abundance of peat, barley, and water, would have started producing rudimentary whisky in home stills, a practice that would grow and eventually change the landscape of Scotland forever.

The first written record of whisky in Scotland pops up much earlier, in Fife in 1494: "To Friar John Cor, of Lindores Abbey being granted eight bolls of malt wherewith to make aqua vitae by order of King James the IV." Another two hundred years would pass before we see any concrete reference to it. You'll notice, should you start studying whiskey history on your own, that there's a worldwide, written-record scarcity when it comes to whiskey. That makes common sense to me, though: I wouldn't record where I hid my profitable goods, how I made my spirit, and how much money I made off of it. I'd do my best to keep it from being taxed by the king or government and stolen by a neighboring clan or invader. I'd pass on a secret recipe to my children, too. Scottish writer Aeneas MacDonald wrote in 1934, "The origin of whiskey is, as it ought to be, hidden in the clouds of mystery that veil the youth of the human race." Take everything you hear, then, with a grain of salt. Lots of it is conjecture (including what you read here).

I've traveled the Highlands dozens of times and what I can tell you with certainty is this: Don't expect any uniform taste when it comes to Scotch from a Highland distillery. You'll discover floral and heathery expressions created by Glenmorangie, which is situated on the lush River Tain in the northeast; while Talisker, built on the lonely Isle of Skye to the west, makes an earthy, salty, peaty whiskey. The Highland Park Distillery, located on the treeless, windswept island of Orkney, embodies florals, vanillas, and smoke.

### Speyside

Speyside is located *within* the Highlands. There are so many distilleries concentrated in this little corner of Scotland that the region deserves its own shout-out. The River Spey, as it is called in Scotland, is both the fastest flowing river and the second longest in the country. The lochs, burns, and streams that keep Speyside green and lush also provide distillers there with an abundance of good water to use for making whisky. Speyside is also strategically placed: It was safer to move whisky through the hills there rather than via the flatter Lowlands bordering England or by sea in the far north.

About half of all single malt Scotch brands are made in distilleries from this small area; the array of flavors and styles created by the distilleries operating there will intrigue you, as it still does me. The Balvenie and Glenfiddich distilleries operate within a five-minute walk from each other, yet you'll be able to identify each distillery's distinct and unique character: The Glenfiddich 12 displays apple and fruit notes and an easy, approachable texture, while The Balvenie carries richer tones of honey, orange, and a bit of spice. If you visit these distilleries, be sure to spend a morning hiking to The Macallan, which is world renowned for its luxurious, sherry-influenced whisky. You'll marvel that these three very different single malts are all made with the same three ingredients (more on that later), but are located so close that they are accessible by foot.

## LET'S TALK ABOUT GLEN

Glenfiddich, GlenDronach, Glenlivet, Glen Fall
I once knew a man who had sampled them all
Glenisla, Glenugie, Glenkinchie, that's plenty
He looked sixty-five, but in fact he was twenty.

George Donald/Buff Hardie, *"Leave Us Our Glens"*

Are "Glen" whiskies all related? Not at all. "Glen" simply means "narrow valley" in Scotland. Many Speyside and Highland whiskies in particular begin their names with "Glen," which gives you an idea of how hilly the landscape is. What follows after "Glen" provides us with a more detailed description of the type of glen in which the distillery sits. The full names of these whiskies are usually old family names or Gaelic words that reflect the environment.

**Glenfiddich:** Valley of the Deer

**Glenmorangie:** Valley by the Forest

**Glenlivet:** Valley Full of Water

**GlenDronach:** Valley of the Blackberries

**Glenrothes:** Valley of the Earl of Rothes (also a town now)

## Lowlands

What's exciting about the Lowlands is the massive industrial-size distilleries that pump out millions of caes of the world's most beloved blended Scotch whiskies, such as Johnnie Walker, Grant's, and Chivas Regal, employing thousands of Scots. Don't get cynical on me here—just because they're gigantic operations doesn't mean they can't be any good— we'll get into that in a bit.

Only three single malt Scotches come from the Lowlands— Glenkinchie, Bladnoch, and Auchentoshan—and that makes it a challenge to describe some sort of overall single malt Scotch Lowland style. I hear people all the time refer to the Lowlands as "light" whiskies. But I find a rich nuttiness in the Auchentoshan Three Wood, which I don't describe as light. It is also the last distillery in Scotland to triple distill its whisky, a practice common in the Lowlands in the nineteenth century. Triple distillation usually means that a whiskey will be lighter, but not always. I put Auchentoshan on my recommended list for you to try so that you can appreciate how wood can override geographical placement, triple distillation, and history in terms of character.

## Campbeltown

Campbeltown sits on the Kintyre Peninsula, which on the Scottish map looks like a finger pointing south toward England. More than thirty different distilleries once operated in Campbeltown, yet today only a mere three remain, from which one of them a very popular whiskey flows: Springbank. They produce brands called Springbank, Hazelburn, and Longrow. All are worth a try should you see any of them on a shelf.

## HOW DO YOU SAY THAT?
### A LESSON IN GAELIC

You may have just breezed over that smattering of letters in the word "Auchentoshan" without trying to sound it out. Let me help you. If you see *ch* in a Gaelic word, pronounce it as you would the *ck* in "clock." That's not exactly how the Scots do it, but close enough, and better than using the *ch* sound as in "*chum*." The Scots actually soften the *ck* sound; they breathe through it and never quite touch the back of the tongue to the roof of the palate to create a hard stop as we do. Now you know how to pronounce Glenfiddich and Loch Ness, in case you were unsure.

## HIGHLANDS VERSUS LOWLANDS

Fun Fact: Highlands and Lowlands do not refer to north and south or higher up on the map and lower on the map. Don't laugh if you already knew that. I get this question all the time. The designation between the Highlands and Lowlands is actually a reference to a geographic fault line called, aptly, the Highland Boundary Fault. In most places, you can actually see the change in geography and topography between the Highlands and Lowlands. As it so happens, the fault line lies on the diagonal across the country. As such, there are some Scottish towns more north that are considered part of the Lowlands.

### Islay

Don't plan on having a hot date with Islay whisky on your tongue—unless your date also enjoys the taste of the oysters, brine, and smoke. I tell this to some of the single men who come to my classes and usually they respond with a polite laugh. Recently, though, a gentleman said, "You know what? If I found a woman who liked that taste, I would marry her instantly. I would follow her forever . . . this will be my test." Passion for whiskies made on Islay runs very deep.

The island of Islay, pronounced *"Eye* luh," lies off the west coast of Scotland and only twenty-five miles north of the Irish coast. You've probably seen some of its world-famous single malts on the shelves of your favorite bar: Laphroaig, Lagavulin, and Ardbeg. Basically, if you can't pronounce the label, chances are it's an Islay. Think Bunnahabhain and Bruichladdich and Caol Ila, too. Nine distilleries currently operate on Islay and most of them share flavors of smoke and peat to varying degrees as measured in ppm. Brands have started releasing special whiskies advertising levels of ppm, beckoning brave souls who like to taste nothing else.

There's more beauty to be found in an Islay whisky than just the smoke and peat. Look for some vanilla and floral notes that lend a bit of unexpected complexity to the Bowmore range, or some sweet pear to balance the dry smoke on the Ardbeg 10. I find that the best Islay whiskies somehow manage to bottle the whole world: the sea, earth, fire, and air. Drink one and be transported to the edge of a rocky craig, salt spray wetting your cheeks, while you quietly look east with nothing between you and Canada.

## PEAT MADNESS TASTING!

The following tasting is a progressive exploration into the world of peated whiskies. I have included a few of my favorites—ones that I think offer a nice balance with other aromas—as well as whiskies that contain the highest ppm currently available.

**PEATED WHISKY TASTING FOR THE CRAZED PEAT FANATIC**

Bunnahabhain (Islay): 1–2 ppm

Hakushu (Japan): 7–8 ppm

Amrut Fusion (India): 23 ppm

Bowmore: 18–25 ppm

Lagavulin: 35–40 ppm

Laphroaig: 40–43 ppm

Talisker: 25–30 ppm

Bruichladdich: 40 ppm

Bruichladdich Octomore: 169 ppm

# SINGLE MALT SCOTCH

There are currently about 105 single malt Scotch distilleries operating in Scotland, and that number changes as distilleries open or close yearly. (A distillery that is closed for a bit of time and then opens again is called "mothballed.")

Let's break down exactly what "single malt Scotch" means by looking at each word individually.

"Single" means one single distillery. It does *not* mean single barrel, single grain, or single cask. It is that simple. Let me say it again, because

this is very confusing: Single means *"one single distillery."* Repeat that
three times.

"Malting" is the process of soaking a grain of barley in water until it
germinates, as we discussed in chapter 2. Once it germinates, distilleries
dry the barley so that the starch is accessible.

## WHERE DO THEY MALT BARLEY?

There are a handful of distilleries that malt on distillery
grounds, in what's called a malt house, but many distilleries buy malts from outside sources. Even the distilleries
that showcase their quaint on-site malting floors often
still subsidize their yield with outside malting facilities—
they just can't make enough malted barley. Don't let this
leave you feeling cold. I've visited these "outside" malting
facilities and still step in mud and pebbles while being
"evil-eyed" by a Highland cow, or "coo" as locals say. It's
still agricultural and romantic just the way you might en-
vision it, so I don't put too much stock in the virtues of
home-ground malting. I heard a story about a whisky
seller at a well-known New York City liquor store harass-
ing a whisky producer about malting on site versus off
site, and whether or not the doors are open in the malt
house to allow natural "yeasts" to fly in. That's all a bit
much if you ask me.

"Scotch" comes from—you guessed it—Scotland. There are a slew
of additional rules a producer must follow for the privilege of printing
the word "Scotch" on the bottle, as I've described above. Namely, that

the whisky must age for a minimum of three years on Scottish soil in oak casks not exceeding 185 pounds (700 liters) and bottled at no less than 40 percent alcohol by volume (80 proof).

There you have it. Single. Malt. Scotch.

## How to Appreciate a Single Malt Scotch

One of the best ways to know what you're getting into with a single malt Scotch is to first read the label—most distillers are darn proud to tell you the types of casks they use, the age, the distillery, region, and how they mature the whisky, too. You'll find clues about whether or not your whisky is chill filtered, finished in a special type of cask, and many other choices distillers make before bottling their whisky (we went over this in chapter 2). You'll know, for example, to expect an oilier or rich whisky if a bottle says "non–chill filtered" on the front, or to look for some fig and raisin notes if it says "aged in ex-Oloroso sherry casks."

Use the list of descriptor words from chapter 1 to see how many you can use, and notice how strongly or timidly each descriptor might spike. For example, I often get vanilla and coconuts in some single malt Scotches, but certainly not to the extent that they pop in an American whiskey that uses new oak. Scotch tastes and noses a bit drier to me compared with American whiskey. I hope you noticed that, too, in your broad tasting.

---

### AGE STATEMENTS

*The age statement on the bottle promises that the whiskey inside was matured for at least the amount of time listed. A whiskey can be older, but not younger, than its age statement.*

---

## Single Malts and Casks

Because approximately 70 percent of the flavor of a single malt Scotch comes from the wood, you'll want to spend a good amount of time exploring how your whisky matured. Most distillers import American ex-bourbon and Spanish ex-sherry casks from which most of the big vibrant wood characteristics have already been extracted. These mellowed and seasoned casks lend a subtlety to whiskies; vanillas and tannins are often refined rather than dominant. Young, nonpeated, ex-bourbon–aged single malt Scotches that have been aged between ten and twelve years are some of my favorite whiskies. I like them because I get to taste all those lighter perfumed notes without new wood, sherried, or smoke notes that can sometimes overwhelm my senses. I throw them on ice in the springtime.

---

*Sláinte means "health" or "cheers" in Gaelic and is pronounced slightly differently depending on where you come from in Ireland or Scotland. Try the Scottish pronunciation, "slawn-jeh," the next time you need to give a wedding toast. There are more Gaelic speakers still living in Scotland than Ireland, believe it or not.*

---

## Single Malt Scotch Tasting Recommendations

Here are some great single malt Scotch whiskies to sample. The Scotches on the list offer innovative cask maturation methods, a good range of styles and ages, and are widely available. And please don't dismiss these big brand names. They get it right. Getting familiar with these whiskies as a base will help you get into more esoteric, rare, and smaller brands down the road. You'll be able to spot real value.

Don't dismiss the younger aged whiskies from these distilleries either. I also chose the distilleries on this list because their youngest expressions, which are often around twelve years old, are very good. My

## MOST SINGLE MALT SCOTCHES TELL YOU EVERYTHING YOU COULD POSSIBLY WANT TO KNOW ABOUT THE LIQUID INSIDE.

**SINGLE MALT SCOTCH:**
Means that the bottle followed a certain set of rules: 1. Produced in Scotland. 2. Aged for a minimum of three years on Scottish soil. 3. Is made with water, yeast, and barley only. 4. Comes from only one distillery. 5. Bottled at a minimum of 40 percent ABV.

**THE BALVENIE:**
Name of distillery.

**BANFFSHIRE:**
Region in which The Balvenie is produced, located in Speyside.

**DOUBLEWOOD:**
Refers to the two types of wood the distillery used for maturation.

**12 YEARS:** The *minimum* amount of time the spirit sat in casks. A promise to you that nothing in the bottle has been aged *less than* twelve years.

**CASK ILLUSTRATION:**
The two types of casks used during maturation: ex-sherry and ex-bourbon.

**43.1% ABV:** The alcohol content contained within.

**DUFFTOWN:** The town where Balvenie is produced.

*The Balvenie bottle*

theory is that if a distillery can't get a young whiskey right, don't bother going much older than that. The twelve-year-olds are closest to what my friend Ian says is the "naked characteristic" of the distillery.

Glenfiddich

The Balvenie

GlenDronach

Auchentoshan

The Macallan (Look for both American and sherry
versions to try; I'm partial to the new oak.)

Scapa

Glenfarclas

Glenmorangie

The Dalmore

Deanston

Cragganmore

Old Pulteney

**Peated**

Oban

Talisker

Highland Park

Ardbeg

Bowmore

Laphroaig

Lagavulin

Bruichladdich

Springbank

Okay, get ready now: The different types of Scotch listed below sound similar. Getting into the details behind what makes a blended malt Scotch whisky and a blended Scotch whisky different might make you dizzy. It's okay to read the descriptions a couple of times to let the differences between these styles become clear—the descriptions are confusing.

## BLENDED SCOTCH WHISKY

Blended Scotch whisky is a blend of whiskies from two or more single malt Scotch distilleries in one bottle. But wait! There is more! Notice that the word "malt" is missing on these labels: Johnnie Walker Black Label Blended Scotch Whisky and Dewar's "White Label" Blended Scotch Whisky. The missing "malt" clues you in that the whiskies are not made from 100 percent barley. They are actually a blend of malt whisky *and* "grain" whisky.

Grain whiskies can consist of corn, wheat, and barley and are produced at six large-production single-grain distilleries that you'll rarely see mentioned by name. These massive distilleries—many located in the Lowlands—churn out large volumes of grain whisky in enormous column stills that maximize output. Later, master blenders marry grain whisky with various malt whiskies to create a balanced spirit that appeals to many palates. Johnnie Walker makes its whiskies this way and tops the list as the best-selling whiskies in the world—I've ordered drams on my travels in Kyoto, Tanzania, Mumbai, and on airplanes getting there.

Blended brands like Dewar's, Chivas, and Johnnie Walker keep their recipes secret. We often don't know the age of the whisky in any given bottle, nor do we know which distilleries we taste or the percentage of grain spirit versus malt whisky used. My best advice if you want to do some sleuthing about a blend's content is to uncover which distilleries the parent company owns. Johnnie Walker's parent company, Diageo, owns single malt Scotch distilleries Talisker, Cragganmore, Cardhu,

Mortlach, Lagavulin, and Oban, among others. So I'd bet money that those whiskies make up a portion of the distilleries used in the Johnnie Walker blends. Last I heard, almost thirty different single malt Scotches make up the Johnnie Walker Black recipe.

Some of you will ask me if blended Scotch whisky is inferior to single malt Scotch whisky. Not so fast—there's an art to harmonizing grain whisky and malt whisky together in a way that appeals to millions of thirsty whisky drinkers worldwide. And these whiskies certainly are very enjoyable at the right time and place. Blended Scotches like Johnnie Walker Black are *easy* to drink, and they don't ask much of you beyond the ten bucks you spend for a glass. You won't find particularly strong flavors or aromas; rather, they are buffed until something clean and smooth emerges. Their quick, thin finish and light texture often make a blended Scotch an ideal aperitif, because it won't overwhelm your palate before a big wine or complex meal is served.

## Blended Malt Scotch Whisky Versus Blended Scotch Whisky

Blended malt Scotch whiskies do exist, but there are only a few you'll be able to find. This style is a blend of two or more single malt Scotch whiskies from different distilleries. The word "malt" is our clue that the bottle contains nothing but barley from the different single malt distilleries—no grain whiskies are involved. Monkey Shoulder, Compass Box Spice Tree, and Sheep Dip are all blended malts that are fun to try, and all three are in my own collection.

Warning: You may find bottles that display the now-banned use of the following blended malt Scotch whisky terms: "vatted malt," "pure malt," and "pure Scotch malt whisky." Producers thought that using the word "blend" devalued the whisky, so they skirted the issue. The Scotch Whisky Association eradicated the use of those terms in 2009 in an effort to make things more clear for you and me. A blend is a blend.

## Single Grain Scotch Whisky

Single grain Scotch whisky is a whiskey made in one single distillery, but using a variety of grains in the mash. A better, less confusing name would be single (distillery) grain whisky.

## Blended Grain Scotch Whisky

Blended grain Scotch whisky is exactly what it sounds like. It is made by blending two or more single grain Scotch whiskies from different distilleries (as opposed to single malt distilleries). I don't make lots of recommendations for you to run out and buy blended grain Scotch whiskies—there just aren't that many. Hedonism by Compass Box and The Snow Grouse, made by The Edrington Group, which also makes Highland Park and The Macallan, are my top picks for blended grain Scotch whisky.

### JOHNNIE WALKER BLUE—
### "WHAT'S THE DEAL?"

I know you want me to answer this question—Johnnie Walker Blue is one of the most widely talked about brands among bankers, golfers, jet-setters, CEOs, lawyers, and anyone else looking to buy a brand that says "I spend money and enjoy the finer things in life." Johnnie Walker Blue is about flash.

At $189 to $200 a bottle, though, many people have asked me what's in it that makes it so expensive. As you now know, because it's a blended Scotch whisky, Johnnie Walker Blue contains a blend of grain Scotch whiskies and single malt Scotch whisky. Johnnie Walker will never fully reveal how long it ages, although each bottle is probably aged somewhere between eighteen and twenty-five years. The heart of the blend supposedly comes from more rare and precious distilleries, including a distillery named Royal Lochnagar.

Johnnie Walker Blue delivers the easy symphony of flavors blended Scotch whisky is famous for: It's a whisky that won't challenge the palate or linger around for a half hour after you sip it. It's an elegant, lighter Scotch, without overwhelming peat and smoke notes. There isn't much not to like about Johnnie Walker Blue—the rub for most of us lies in its cost and whether or not we can get a better value whisky. But few brands send the same *bling* message that Johnnie Walker Blue does.

## Blended Scotch Shopping List

My favorite blended whisky brands, based on availability and value, are the following. And to bring music back into the conversation, my friend Robin Robinson, who is the whisky ambassador to Compass Box, offers up a most helpful analogy between appreciating blended and single malt whiskies: "Blendeds are a symphony orchestra with all the instruments mingling together in acoustic harmony. Single malts are a jazz band—you might get some wonderful notes popping out here and there."

Dewar's 12 (blended Scotch whisky)
Johnnie Walker Black (blended Scotch whisky)
Compass Box Spice Tree (blended malt Scotch whisky)
Monkey Shoulder (blended malt Scotch whisky)
The Snow Grouse (blended grain Scotch whisky)
Compass Box Hedonism (blended grain Scotch whisky)

# THE BIG AMERICAN WHISKEY SLAP DOWN

*Whiskey distilleries now dot the American landscape from coast to coast. While bourbon can be made anywhere in the U.S.A., Kentucky has long been the spiritual heartland.*

Recently, two hedge-fund managers sitting on The Flatiron Room bar stools demanded that I procure *either* a bottle of Black Maple Hill or Pappy Van Winkle for them. (They also mentioned discreetly that I'd be paid handsomely for the task.) When I informed them I had neither American whiskey in my supposed "secret stash," they accused me of either lying or hoarding. It took a while for me to convince them of this unbelievable truth: We run out of many American whiskey brands these days. It happens a lot. In this country, our love for whiskey is so strong now that on May 22, 2013, the 226-year-old historic American whiskey distiller Buffalo Trace put out a press release informing its thirsty fans that demand now officially outstripped supply—whiskies such as Eagle Rare, W. L. Weller, Blanton's, and even Buffalo Trace, their flagship brand, were selling out faster than they can distill and bottle them. Glassware maker Libbey celebrated record sales of more than $800 million, partly because of the demand for its brown spirits collection. In 2012, whiskey sales outpaced vodka, gin, tequila, and other spirits, according to an alcohol industry trade group, the Distilled Spirits Council of the United States (DISCUS).

The gutsiest move to heed the American whiskey cause, though, came from Maker's Mark, which thought that adding a bit of water before bottling would help increase supply and appease angry, empty-handed fans. Instead, bloggers, reporters, and Maker's Mark loyalists stomped and screamed, "Give us back our whiskey!" After having taken the whiskey down three percentage points to 42 percent ABV, the company went back to the original 45 percent very quickly.

Why the tremendous growth? Bartenders have certainly stimulated our whiskey palates by embracing and playing with flavors, introducing us to the craft of mixing a good drink. "Mixology" bars popped up in just about every major city during the past decade, and I bet you have a few favorite bars like I do. Hollywood fueled the whiskey flames by introducing us to vintage sexpots like Don Draper in *Mad Men*, who kept a couple of bottles of whiskey in his office. The rise of bespoke suit shops, pork pie hats, suspenders, locally sourced food, and the popularity of salt-of-the-earth folksy bands like Mumford & Sons are a few more cultural elements that point to our love of an era in which whiskey was king among all spirits. I, too, have my own vintage glassware, 1960s dress collection, and a weakness for brands that weave stories of authenticity and provenance into their brand history. This makes me weak for American whiskey, as it does many of you. But I want to pull back the curtain and get beyond the pop-culture marketing gloss. When we talk about whiskey in America, we need to start with something very unromantic: the TTB.

The Alcohol and Tobacco Tax and Trade Bureau, a branch of the government that regulates labeling and advertising in American whiskey, protects definitions of whiskey so that your uncle in Denmark can't make bourbon—our most popular style of American whiskey—and sell it as such in the United States. It also enforces labeling rules so that, for example, if you want to call your bottle of whiskey bourbon, you'll need to oblige a bunch of parameters in order to do so. To understand what's in the vast number of American whiskeys being made today, I rely on the current set of TTB rules laid out for each style of whiskey, and then look at a label for more clues. But as you'll see, with American whiskey, it's often what's left *unsaid* that will help you decipher a bottle's contents. Let's get to the bottom of that before getting into the particulars of each American whiskey's style.

### Reading the Whiskey Label:
### Non-Distiller Producers—What's Left Unsaid

In terms of naming and labeling, American whiskey is not like the Scotch whisky world. For example, The Balvenie Distillery makes The Balvenie Scotch and names the individual types The Balvenie 12, 15, and so on. Simple, right? Not so with American whiskey. A big distillery like Buffalo Trace can make all sorts of brands, such as Eagle Rare, Blanton's, and W. L. Weller. Some distilleries even sell whiskeys to what are now commonly called non-distiller producers (NDPs). NDPs then sell the whiskey under a different label after either tweaking flavors through chill filtration, dilution, or mingling casks or reselling it after doing nothing but repackaging it. Your job is to read the text on the bottle. When you read "produced by," "bottled by," "handmade," or "hand bottled by" *without* the term "distilled by," then that is a clue the bottle might be sold by an NDP. Not always, though. There are some small distilleries that don't actually put "distilled by" on the bottle, even if they have distilled it. I think they should put it on the bottle, and as more consumers ask "Where is my whiskey distilled?" you'll start to see most distilleries list that on the label. Another clue to look for is whether or not the "bottled in" state is the same as the "distilled in" state. When they're different, that's another clue that the whiskey is NDP. The TTB regulates what can be called a bourbon, rye, corn whiskey, and so on, but not where your whiskey is actually distilled or comes from *within* the United States.

The number of brands available on the shelf has always outnumbered the operating distilleries that exist. That's legal, and I don't have a problem with this centuries-old practice. The concept of the NDP seriously irks some whiskey fans, though—just Google "NDP" and watch out for the daggers. NDP opponents claim that brands are being sneaky and trying to deceive you—that they should describe whether or not they distilled it, and if not, list who did. But I'm teaching you to be a great whiskey connoisseur. Deceiving you is no longer easy.

Now that we've covered NDPs, let's move on to what we can all agree on—what styles American whiskey makers produce.

## BOURBON!

You've gone and done it. You've expressed a preference for bourbon within earshot of another person. Little did you realize that arguing about bourbon is now our sixth most popular sport, behind arguing about "grape vs. grain" vodkas, parenting strategies, craft beers, workout regimens, and college football.

—"How to Win Any Bourbon Argument," *Esquire*, August 9, 2013

The definition of bourbon is something we don't need to argue, as Congress set the parameters on May 4, 1964, about what makes the spirit "a distinctive product of the United States." Here's the quick and dirty rundown:

- Bourbon is an American spirit. Only America. Not France, not China. America.
- Bourbon can be made anywhere in the U.S.A., legally. There are bourbons from dozens of states. Spiritually? That's up to you. My friends in Kentucky call their home state holy ground for whiskey. When I'm there and they're buying, I don't argue. Don't you argue, either.
- Bourbon can be called bourbon only if the mash bill (grain makeup) is at least 51 percent corn. The other 49 percent can be any other grain. In fact, the whiskey maker can even use 100 percent corn, if he wants to.
- When the mash bill consists of a high concentration of rye as the second ingredient, we call it *high-rye bourbon*. Rye gives a dry and spicy character to whiskey.
- When the mash bill consists of a high concentration of wheat as a second ingredient, we call that a *wheated bourbon*. Wheated bourbon can drink sweeter, a little like white chocolate or rock candy. But you'll see for yourself.
- Bourbon must be aged in charred new oak. It does not matter for how long. Stick it in a barrel and blink twice or wait until your marriage disintegrates. Whatever. Take it out. That's bourbon! Don't want to put it in a barrel? That's not bourbon. That's unaged bourbon, or white dog. You can do that, too, but don't call it bourbon.
- Bourbon must be distilled at no higher than 160 proof (80 percent ABV).
- Bourbon must be put into the barrel at no higher than 125 proof (62.5 percent ABV). But the lower the proof at the time of a barrel

fill, the better I think it will taste at the end of maturation (see casking in chapter 2).

- Bourbon must be bottled at a minimum of 80 proof (40 percent ABV). Seem strong, vodka drinkers? When you say you can't drink whiskey because it's "too strong and I get too drunk," remember that the spirit you're drinking is very close to or even the same ABV as most whiskeys listed in this book.

- "Straight" bourbon whiskey, which you'll see a lot on the labels, is a term for whiskey matured in charred new American oak barrels for a minimum of two years.

---

### WHISKEY FACTS DISTILLED

Yes! Bourbon can be made *anywhere* in the United States!

---

## No One Invented Bourbon

Here's the big bourbon reveal: Bourbon was not "invented." What we now know today as bourbon is the cumulative result of almost two millennia of spirit making, and we still fine-tune and tweak it. Trying to find out who invented bourbon feels a bit like looking into who invented the modern hammer. You'll start unwinding details of a hammer's history until you find yourself reading about tools used in the middle of the Paleolithic Stone Age, when sticks wrapped with animal skins were attached to stones for pounding and breaking things. While whiskey's not *that* old, it's still considered ancient: Distillation will bring you back at least two thousand years, as we discussed in chapter 2.

Early American settlers from France, England, Germany, Spain, Scotland, and Ireland, then, had already practiced distillation in their mother countries by the time they arrived. In France, a theologian and doctor named Arnaud de Villeneuve had distilled wine by the end of the thirteenth century. In Ireland the monks were possibly distilling by the fifth century; as early as 1437, Germany was distilling "burned water" (brandy); and Scotland had been distilling soon after the Irish missionaries landed there to convert them to Christianity. For both medicinal purposes and profit making, rudimentary home distilling was as common as growing corn and keeping a couple of cows.

The art of building casks for storage—called coopering—is downright ancient, too, while we're at it. An Egyptian tomb dated 2690 BC reveals a painting of a straight-sided tublike vessel held together with wooden hoops. Christopher Columbus's crew on the *Santa Maria* included Domingo Vizcaino, whose role was to keep food and liquids from leaking out of casks, and to build new ones as needed. I don't mean to take away from America's contribution to the whiskey world; I merely point out that we didn't really invent distillation, or the idea of storing perishable goods in a new cask either, essential elements of what makes a bourbon a bourbon.

### Why Is Kentucky So Famous for Bourbon?

American frontiersman Daniel Boone made his way to what we now call Kentucky in 1767, and by the early 1800s, more than two thousand whiskey barrels were shipped out of Kentucky via Ohio River ports to faraway settlements like New Orleans. In Kentucky, an abundance of trees for casks, a carpet of fertile soil for growing corn, access to iron-free waters for whiskey making, the convergence of rivers for shipping, and a climate that allowed casks to expand in heat and contract in the cold all mingled together in a perfect storm to make Kentucky America's spiritual home base for whiskey. Taxation, the Civil War, cheap imitators, Prohibition, and World War II all threatened Kentucky's bourbon industry—sometimes bringing it to its knees—but like a trick candle, no one blow snuffed it out completely. Today Kentucky produces 95 percent of all bourbon.

The most popular legend as to how bourbon got its name comes out of Kentucky as well. The story goes something like this: Imbibers in New Orleans loved the taste of whiskey coming off of boats in casks stamped with the phrase "From Limestone, Bourbon County, Kentucky." The casks would have taken months to get to New Orleans on a flatboat, ample time for the wood to smooth the rough corn whiskey edge. Soon whiskey fans down south along the rivers were ordering the spirit by its shortened name, "Give me a bourbon!"

My friend and whiskey historian Michael Veach disagrees, though, and tells me that the long journey and limited trade wouldn't have attracted enough buzz for the term "bourbon" to catch on. His theory is that a couple of sharp businessmen—two French brothers—set up a warehouse along the river, established trade with New Orleans, and aged whiskey before sending it down the river. They called their whiskey bourbon, knowing how nice it sounded to the French immigrants in Louisiana. I'm fine with your reciting either one of these two stories at your next cocktail party.

### THIRSTY FOR MORE BOURBON HISTORY?

Michael Veach loves to put shiny bourbon legends and stories to rest. His book *Kentucky Bourbon Whiskey: An American Heritage* is a great read if you want to get into a 130-page detailed look at bourbon's past. I tooled around with him one day in his Jeep filled with pipe-tobacco ashes, discussing bourbon legends (and classic rock bands) as we drove along a Kentucky highway toward Jim Beam in Bardstown from Louisville. We had started our day by eating the same thing President Harry Truman enjoyed for breakfast every morning: one egg, one piece of toast, one slice of bacon, one fruit cup, one glass of milk, and one shot of Old Grand-Dad bourbon.

## What Makes Tasty Bourbon?

As you taste different bourbons, popular whiskey aromatics will appear: vanillas, caramels, tannins, maple, almonds, dark cherries, and other cask-driven notes. What you are looking for, then, are differences in the flavor "spikes" and subtleties that waft in different degrees in the brands. You should also look for notes that you personally prefer, and start making your own judgments as you experiment.

Bourbons run the gamut from soft wheated bourbons to shots of spicy high-rye bourbons. There is a bourbon for every mood and occasion. For example, when I'm looking for a whiskey with strong vanilla notes, a short finish, and a somewhat floral or springtime personality, I'll grab a whiskey with a mash bill consisting of plenty of wheat (wheated bourbon) like Rebel Yell or something from the Weller line. These are both fairly young whiskeys (when there's no age statement, that's one shiny clue) with a wheated mash bill that tastes softer and sweeter on my palate than a high-rye bourbon like the Four Roses small batch whiskey. I'd order something like the Four Roses on a damp, rainy November evening after stopping in at a local bar with friends on my way home from work. Bourbons with a more typical mash bill, such as the Buffalo Trace bourbon (a brand made at the distillery with the same name), lie somewhere in between.

Some bourbons may nose very similarly, but will have distinct textures or finish—some might linger longer on the back palate and down your throat, or some might feel much creamier. Sometimes bourbons hit some of our bitter receptors, which we talked about in chapter 1, but one hopes not too strongly or harshly—just enough to excite our tongues. Balance is tricky. New oak drives an enormous amount of wood into a whiskey, so it is difficult even for skilled whiskey makers to capture more structured, puckery notes without making them overpowering. Tannins do that, and a little tannin is very nice. Aged whiskeys like the Elijah Craig 12 and Michter's 10 do a nice job giving a bit of that tannin and subtle wood-char aroma in addition to those expected bourbon aromas like spice, vanilla, and caramel.

Age, mash bill (sometimes listed on the bottle, but not always), and ABV percentage will all intermingle to create a whiskey's individual whiskey character, so again, look at your bottle and discern as much as you can.

## THE UNICORN OF AMERICAN WHISKEY: PAPPY VAN WINKLE

No whiskey has captured the American imagination as much as the elusive Pappy Van Winkle. The brand story is filled with just enough broken dreams and resurrections to make a phoenix beam with envy—and Americans love stories that mirror the rough-and-tumble fantasy of our pioneers. Many of us also appreciate a tough challenge—Pappy Van Winkle hunting has become a pastime in some circles. Adding more to the mystique, a 2013 theft of more than seventy cases of Pappy made headline news, with a $10,000 reward offered up by the Bluegrass Crime Stoppers and an anonymous donor. While you are more likely to grow a tail than land a bottle of Pappy for your bar, the buzz and hype around the brand make it impossible to ignore.

Here's Pappy's history in a snapshot: In 1893 a young gentleman by the name of Julian "Pappy" Van Winkle began working as a salesman for liquor wholesaler W. L. Weller & Sons. Julian bought Weller, and then later partnered with Stitzel, the distillery that supplied them with liquor. The company Stitzel-Weller came together after Prohibition, selling delicious wheated bourbon when Pappy was sixty-one years old. Stitzel operated during Prohibition under a special "medicinal" license given them to continue making whiskey, so the distillery was never put to rest like so many others.

Prohibition silenced Stitzel and Weller for a little while, but oddly, it wasn't until the advent of the 1970s that Stitzel-Weller really fell on hard times. Feisty boomers saw bourbon as something their parents drank. And think about it: When you picture the late 1960s, early 1970s, don't you picture pot and groovy mai tai cocktails? Whiskey sales tanked.

In 1972, the Van Winkle family sold Stitzel-Weller under the condition that Julian Jr., Pappy's son, could procure old whiskey stocks from the Stitzel-Weller distillery and keep the name Van Winkle. Julian and his brand Old Rip Van Winkle hobbled along for the next three decades, and the Stitzel-Weller site fell into ruins after changing hands many times and getting swallowed up by bigger and bigger companies, finally closing shop in 1991.

Today, the Buffalo Trace Distillery in Kentucky makes a range of Pappy whiskeys in partnership with the Van Winkle family, using the family's original wheated mash bill recipe. Some of the old Stitzel-Weller Pappy can be found at auctions or through eBay, but you'll pay dearly—rumor has it that the old Stitzel-Weller Distillery made some of the best bourbons ever produced, and many fans are prepared to pony up for a bottle.

# HOW TO READ A BOTTLE OF AMERICAN BOURBON

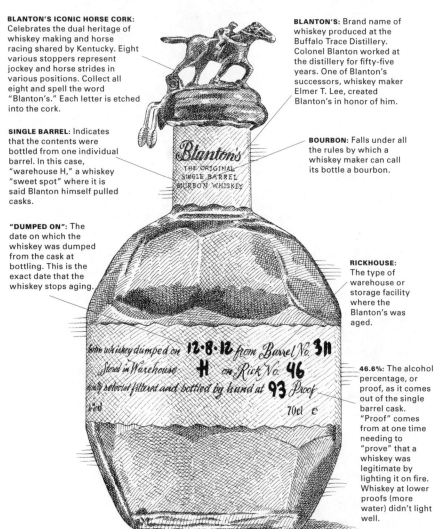

**BLANTON'S ICONIC HORSE CORK:** Celebrates the dual heritage of whiskey making and horse racing shared by Kentucky. Eight various stoppers represent jockey and horse strides in various positions. Collect all eight and spell the word "Blanton's." Each letter is etched into the cork.

**SINGLE BARREL:** Indicates that the contents were bottled from one individual barrel. In this case, "warehouse H," a whiskey "sweet spot" where it is said Blanton himself pulled casks.

**"DUMPED ON":** The date on which the whiskey was dumped from the cask at bottling. This is the exact date that the whiskey stops aging.

**BLANTON'S:** Brand name of whiskey produced at the Buffalo Trace Distillery. Colonel Blanton worked at the distillery for fifty-five years. One of Blanton's successors, whiskey maker Elmer T. Lee, created Blanton's in honor of him.

**BOURBON:** Falls under all the rules by which a whiskey maker can call its bottle a bourbon.

**RICKHOUSE:** The type of warehouse or storage facility where the Blanton's was aged.

**46.6%:** The alcohol percentage, or proof, as it comes out of the single barrel cask. "Proof" comes from at one time needing to "prove" that a whiskey was legitimate by lighting it on fire. Whiskey at lower proofs (more water) didn't light well.

**NOTE:** No age statement is posted on the Blanton's bottle. Some whiskeys do post the age. We know that it is aged a minimum of two years when it's labeled "straight," but after that, it's the distiller's discretion when to bottle that whiskey. For Blanton's, that's most likely two to six years. No age statement means that it is at least four years old.

*Blanton's bottle*

## Bourbon Brand Tasting Recommendations

TRADITIONAL MASH BILL BOURBON

Elijah Craig 12

Woodford Reserve

Eagle Rare

Wild Turkey

Michter's

Angel's Envy

WHEATED BOURBON

W. L. Weller

Maker's Mark

Old Fitzgerald

Rebel Yell

Larceny

HIGH-RYE BOURBON

Very Old Grand-Dad

Four Roses

Bulleit

Buffalo Trace

Old Forester

# RYE

The first American president is not only notorious in whiskey history for enraging farm distillers with his whiskey tax in 1791, spurring the violent Whiskey Rebellion, but ironically, George Washington was making whiskey at Mount Vernon *at the same time.* His was a rye, with a mash bill of 60 percent rye, 30 percent corn, and 10 percent barley. Thanks to his meticulous record keeping, former Maker's Mark master distiller

Dave Pickerell and Kings County distiller Nicole Austin have resurrected Washington's recipe and methods to create the Mount Vernon rye whiskey that George himself would have enjoyed while discussing whom to tax. It's a rough-around-the-edges, spicy, dry, and rustic-tasting white whiskey that will make your eyes water. You can buy it at Mount Vernon, but other than that I'm not sure which states import the brand.

Rye is the bad boy of grains: It's big, spicy, and can grow well under poor soil conditions, cold weather, and snow. Rye grows in many parts of Europe, too, making it one of the first go-to grains colonials would have tried to grow and eventually distill. For these two reasons, rye was the most popular type of grain early farmers distilled with regularity. Western Pennsylvania—Pittsburgh, specifically—served as ground zero for rye whiskey production in the 1700s with a style called Monongahela, a powerhouse of a drink made with 100 percent rye. Five thousand stills were churning out Monongahela by 1780, and by the end of the 1800s, Pennsylvania distillers produced millions of gallons of the prized spirit.

Prohibition came and shut down the party. It devastated the rye whiskey industry and pushed Americans to adjust their palates toward the bootlegged, softer Canadian whiskies. After repeal, the last remaining rye drinkers sank into the dark corners of dusty old-man bars for a while and a new generation of drinkers celebrated with colorful cocktails. The folk song "Rye Whiskey" by Tex Ritter pretty much sums up the image of the unfashionable 1936 post-Volstead rye imbiber in a nine-stanza song with a hard-luck, down-and-out rye theme:

> *Her parents don't like me, they say I'm too poor*
> *They say I'm unworthy to enter her door*
> *It's a whiskey, rye whiskey, rye whiskey I cry*
> *If I don't get rye whiskey, well, I think I will die*

But American rye sings a sad song no more, lifted out of a dank depression by bartenders who've been pouring the spicy spirit into well-crafted cocktails both old and new, such as the trusty old-fashioned or the one-of-a-kind Autumn Poet (see the recipes in chapter 5). The spicy, robust, and drier aspects of the grain impart a complexity to the bottled spirit that bartenders—and myself—around the United States find irresistible in cocktails or sipped neat.

The rules for when a spirit can be called rye and the bottle guidelines are the same as those for bourbon, with one crucial difference: Instead of using corn as the 51 percent base grain, the distiller substitutes rye. Again, you'll look for all those big new American wood properties in the profile. And as with all whiskeys, inspect the labels for your "what's in it" and "what should I expect" clues (again, some of them are age statement, ABV, straight versus nonstraight, and mash bill recipe— not always included).

---

### RYE, AMERICA'S ISLAY? NOT QUITE!

*For lack of a better comparison, some whiskey resources describe American rye whiskey as "America's Islay." Make no mistake: Rye whiskey is nothing, I mean nothing, like the briny, peaty, Islay whisky from Scotland.*

---

I drink rye for the aromatic spice and the dryness—sometimes bitterness—I get across my tongue from the grain's properties. It's a nice juxtaposition with all that sweetness coming out of fresh American oak. Orange, citrus, green, and florals are a few of the other notes I find mouthwatering in a lush rye. But I know people whom I respect tremendously who claim that they don't like rye very much at all. I suspect that human variability when it comes to bitter receptors (as I described in chapter 1) is at play when it comes to rye, because it does have some bitterness to it. You'll have to taste a few to see for yourself if you like it.

Another way to ace the difference between rye and bourbon is to pour some ryes and bourbons side by side and taste them back-to-back.

You'll notice stronger pepper, spice, and grassy notes coming off rye, especially when compared with wheated bourbons, for example. After tasting them, you'll also probably notice the dry feeling on the back of your tongue and down your throat that comes after sipping a rye.

## Rye Shopping List

High West Rendezvous

WhistlePig 10 or 12 (rye casks sourced from Canada)

Bulleit

Rittenhouse

Knob Creek Rye

Michter's

Masterson's 10 (a bit pricey, but very delicious)

Russell's Reserve 6

Old Potrero

# AMERICAN SINGLE MALT WHISKEY

Move over, Scotland, there's a new single malt in town. American whiskey makers—especially new, smaller distilleries looking for ways to differentiate themselves from the big Kentucky guys—are now making whiskeys using malted barley, just as the single malt Scotch makers do. And lucky you—no need to study up on any new TTB regulations—all the American whiskey rules apply (you know the deal now). This time, distillers must throw at least 51 percent malted barley into that mash bill. The result is a uniquely American spin that tastes nothing like single malt Scotch from Scotland, or even Ireland. American single malts often drink young and raw and are tinged with a bit of rustic charm. Put them in a lineup against the Celtic greats and you might use the words "odd" or "strong" to describe the unusual combination of the barley grain and new wood.

There aren't many American single malts to try just yet, but I include them in the book because you'll start seeing more and more of them proliferate on the shelves, and a few of them are tasty in an oddball way. For fun, compare one of the recommended American single malt whiskeys with a young single malt Scotch whisky that you like. Or, during your Scotch tasting (see page 96), substitute an American single malt to see how the regional differences in production really change the flavor of the spirit—Balcones Texas Single Malt is a good one to try because they use 100 percent malted barley and they stumped whiskey panelists during a 2012 blind tasting. Some of the experts thought it was a spectacular and unusual single malt. Another interesting tasting is to try the entire range of an American single malt whiskey, bourbon, and rye produced by a single distillery. This highlights how the differences in grain change a whiskey's flavor because most of the other flavor-making production elements will have been the same. Tuthilltown Spirits distillery in upstate New York makes all three.

### American Single Malt Shopping List

Pine Barrens Single Malt

Balcones Single Malt

Hudson Single Malt

St. George Single Malt

Wasmund's

McCarthy's Oregon Single Malt Whiskey

Devil's Share Single Malt Whiskey

Pearse Lyons Single Malt Whiskey

Defiant American Single Malt Whiskey

## CORN WHISKEY

Corn whiskey has its own special definition within the American whiskey sphere: The mash bill must be made with 80 percent corn and is matured in used or uncharred barrels only. I've seen corn whiskey both white in color and tinged in light gold. Georgia Moon, sold in canning jars, is probably the most famous one you can buy around town.

Balcones Distillery in Texas, in particular, has been leading the corn whiskey innovation charge and playing with different styles of corn to create an incredible array of flavors. In doing so, it has won numerous awards for taste. Along with cask notes such as vanilla, coconut, and spice, you'll taste some of the fired Texas scrub oak and locally grown blue Hopi corn in their Brimstone whiskey, for example—probably one of the few whiskeys we can really think of as expressing terroir. Pure Texan terroir.

### Corn Whiskey Shopping List
Balcones Brimstone
Balcones Baby Blue
Buffalo Trace White Dog Corn Whiskey
Hudson New York Corn
Georgia Moon

### AMERICAN WHISKEY VERSUS SCOTCH WHISKY

You wanted to ask, no?

Here's the big secret: Scotches aren't better than American whiskeys or vice versa. I won't let you become a one-category-only whiskey lover! Whiskey is like beer. If you were on the beach in Mexico, you probably wouldn't reach for a deep and syrupy Guinness freshly poured into a pint glass (as you would in a dark and cozy pub). Instead, you'd probably sip a Corona with a wedge of lime tucked into the bottle. There are simply different experiences that call for different beverages. Whiskey is just as varied. There's a whiskey for every date, time, holiday, season, and occasion.

New whiskey drinkers often describe American whiskey as "strong." Strong usually translates to an instant overwhelming of one's senses, an alcoholic burn. It can also sometimes describe the robust woody notes found in American whiskey, especially when the whiskeys are in a lineup with single malts. American whiskey generally comes into its prime earlier than single malts do—it doesn't sit in a cask for years mellowing out. Instead, it reaches out and grabs you—"Hello! Pay attention to me!"—with its bold flavors. These flavors reveal themselves after the drinker noses and tastes "through" the alcohol proof to get at all those beautiful aromas like coconut, vanilla, and toffee. American whiskey also teaches us that younger whiskeys are vibrant and exciting. They bust the tired myth that "older is better."

## SO YOU WANNA MAKE "WHISKEY" IN YOUR OWN KITCHEN?

It's illegal! It's called making moonshine—which by law isn't even considered whiskey, when it comes right down to it. Moonshine by definition is, very simply, illegally distilled alcohol. But you'll see the name on bottles everywhere anyway because it's fun, catchy, and folksy. It's not illegal to put the word "moonshine" on your bottle, but it's illegal to make it on your own behind the government's back. Still, if prison time and a $10,000 fine don't scare you, there is a great book on how to make moonshine secretly and on your own: *Moonshiners Manual* by Michael Barleycorn. It explains in detail exactly what it is and how to make it with things like lobster pots and grain feed without killing yourself. Moonshine is traditionally made with sugar and a very small percentage of corn, but because no rules exist, a distiller can use whatever's in the kitchen cabinet. I've read about fusel oils, blue vitriol, and zinc salts as some of the messy poisonous by-products of "mountain dew" done wrong. So watch out. And if you're even offered some by your kooky new neighbor? Take heed! Cheap rotgut made with used-car parts like radiators as condensers creates a particularly bad case of popskull—a bad post-moonshine headache—or even insanity. So take a pass on that, too, unless you know your whiskey maker *really* well.

Historically, farmers making whiskey used their excess corn or rye reserves, especially during the half century following George Washington's whiskey tax repeal (thanks, Thomas Jefferson!) in the 1800s. During that time, whiskey drinking flourished, and by 1830, Americans were consuming five to seven gallons of alcohol per year, three times more than today. The belief in alcohol's medicinal qualities combined with tainted water in early settlements made America very wet. Soaked, you might say.

Ensuing conflicts like the Civil War, a growing temperance movement, and the formation of that little-known government agency we now officially call the IRS (since 1953) seriously put a damper on the whiskey fest, driving legal whiskey makers underground and turning them into moonshiners and lawless backwoods saviors for the seriously thirsty.

## "Why Am I Seeing White Whiskey Everywhere? What Is It?"

The term "white whiskey," or "unaged whiskey," is tricky to define. The TTB states that in order for something to be called whiskey, it should at least "have the taste, aroma, and characteristics generally attributed to whiskey." That leaves a lot open to interpretation: How long in oak? Is white whiskey demonstrating characteristics generally attributed to whiskey? Shouldn't whiskey technically be aged in wood? White whiskey proliferation has spurred quite a philosophical debate over the past couple of years.

Selling white whiskey helps growing small distillers make a little money until the aged spirit comes to fruition, and this is partly why you now find white whiskey all over the place—hundreds of new small distilleries were born in the decade between 2003 and 2013. Instead of putting the whole spirit run into casks, distillers siphon off a bit and bottle the "new make" for consumption. Technically, new make is supposed to be aged in oak casks, but some distillers don't do this. Again, the regulations aren't very clear on this point, and to date I haven't seen much enforcement by the government.

Whatever the new distillery hopes to bottle down the line out of casks—bourbon or rye, for example—you can expect that the white whiskey it bottles will contain the exact same mash bill. White dog, white whiskey, white lightning, white rye, unaged whiskey, ghost whiskey, and of course moonshine—you'll see any number of these names used to describe the clear spirit a distiller bottles right off the still.

White American whiskey tastes sweet on the tongue, releases strong mash grain aromatics, puckers your lips, and warms you up. Some of the notes of white whiskey I've experienced are cotton candy, bubble gum, and pine tree, not necessarily in that order. I've recently tasted a white whiskey from the George Dickel Distillery that smells more like buttered popcorn than any whiskey I've ever tasted. White whiskeys make fun ingredients for cocktails, too.

### Moonshine Shopping List
Corsair Pumpkin Spice Moonshine
Death's Door White Whisky
Koval's Rye White Whiskey
King's County Moonshine
Troy & Sons Platinum Heirloom Whiskey

## THE NEW AMERICAN
## WHISKEY MAKERS

Everything just looked old, farty, stale, tired, and corporate.
I wanted something NEW!
DAREK BELL, COFOUNDER/DISTILLER, CORSAIR DISTILLERY,
WHISKY ADVOCATE, AUGUST 2013

In 2004, approximately 63 small distilleries dotted the American landscape, lonely pioneers resurrecting a long-lost craft practiced by just a few giants in Kentucky. A few of them got creative—why make what the big Kentucky bourbon distillers already do so well? Clear Creek Distillery in Oregon distills whiskey in old French-style eau-de-vie stills commonly used for fruit brandies. Chip Tate, who runs Balcones Distilling in Texas, smokes his Brimstone brand of whiskey using a "secret process" that evokes evenings sitting by a campfire after nosing and tasting it. At the Corsair Distillery, Darek Bell mashes quinoa, buckwheat, and amaranth, smoking them with various fruitwoods and hardwoods. This is the new world of American whiskey making.

Today more than 292 distilleries produce some form of whiskey in forty-eight different states. Whiskey making "hot spots" follow the same pattern craft brewers did in the 1990s, with places like Colorado and California leading the way. I believe we are in a bit of a bourbon bubble right now, though, with the explosion of whiskey start-ups mirroring the uptick in whiskey love and desire for artisanal goods. The issue is that whiskey start-ups cost money to build and to run, so when the economy begins to shake, small distillers relying on investment will flutter and fall, much like small beer breweries did after the financial bubble burst in the early 2000s. Don't worry, though: The good news is that the quality whiskeys produced by well-run distilleries will rise to the top. I predict that all the small distillers I include in this book will make it through the long haul. There are others, too, but who survives may be largely up to your wallet.

Take advantage of the whiskey gold rush happening—go find out what small distillery makes whiskey near you and have a poke around. You'll see whiskey innovation and passion at work: Small distillers love playing with different grains and barrel sizes. Economic necessities are a catalyst for innovation, and "happy accidents" are the golden nuggets a distiller depends upon. Cask experimentation lies at the heart of a small distillery operation—a traditional bourbon barrel is fifty-three gallons in size, but getting whiskey out the door at a wee distillery often means maturation in something smaller, thus creating more surface-to-spirit contact. This accelerates maturation and the distillery is able to start selling the whiskey fairly quickly. What you might find is that small-cask matured, young whiskeys lend a too-bitter quality because the influx of all those tannins into the spirit overpowers the subtleties of notes that develop over time in larger casks. I've enjoyed small-cask matured, young whiskeys, and I've tasted some doozies. Tuthilltown Spirits in New York coaxes the intermingling of wood and spirit by playing bass-heavy East Coast hip-hop through subwoofers. They call it "sonic maturation"—the idea is that the vibrations agitate the whiskey like a ripple effect, increasing color and aroma.

### Why Small Distillery Bottles Cost More Money

Small distillers don't enjoy the benefits of "economy of scale" that large distilleries do—they certainly aren't buying massive amounts of corn the way Buffalo Trace does, for example. I scour new whiskey labels for the words "distilled by" so that I know I'm paying a premium price for a grain-to-bottle producer that while making whiskey may also support a local economy with new jobs. Balcones Distilling buys corn from local farmers while other distilleries, like Hillrock Estate Distillery in New York and Clear Creek Distillery in Oregon, grow their own grain. Some NDP producers are building distilleries and sell at a premium to bridge costs. That's cool with me, too. I ask what I'm paying for most when I come across a whiskey brand that outsources all the whiskey and has no plans for a distillery. In that case, I'm looking for something very special or unique about that whiskey, and it better be more than the jaded and cloudy notion of "craft."

### What Is Craft?

Whiskey insiders—which you are now—argue over what constitutes a "craft" whiskey. Does the term "craft" refer to the ratio of workers on site to gallons produced? Is it the presence of an actual distillery, or can an NDP also call itself "craft"? Is it a certain number of cases produced? Is it merely a sentiment or a vibe? Big marketing dollars exploit the term "craft," a term I believe generally applies to small distilleries hand-making whiskey. They'll use the term because too many consumers (not you now!) equate craft with quality or better-tasting whiskey. Don't fall for that idea. Big distilleries have an advantage—they can draw on a large inventory of aged stocks and generations of experience to create a variety of flavors. Ask yourself these two questions: Do I like this whiskey? Can I afford it? From there go ahead and explore provenance.

### Small Distiller Shopping List

Kings County (bourbon, rye, moonshine)

High West (mostly rye)

Balcones (bourbon, corn, single malt)

Long Island Spirits (Rough Rider Bourbon, Pine Barrens Single Malt)

Catskill Distilling (bourbon, rye, wheat whiskey)

Hillrock Estate Distillery (bourbon, single malt)
Westland Distillery (single malt)
Clear Creek (McCarthy's Single Malt)
Widow Jane Whiskey (made from rye mash)
St. George Spirits
Tuthilltown Spirits

## JACK DANIEL'S

I can't write a whiskey book without devoting some space to a brand that is enjoyed by cowboys, buried with Frank Sinatra, sipped by that funny dog on *Family Guy*, hand-drawn on the cover of Mötley Crüe's trashy autobiography, and used as toothpaste by Ke$ha. Jack Daniel's sold 10.6 million cases in 2011, and at least one of those bottles ended up at my house. Don't think I'm beyond Jack Daniel's—none of us is. It's a good whiskey—perfect on ice at a summer cocktail party or with friends in a dive bar. It's been served to me on a silver tray at a wedding in the Hamptons and by a hippie waiter who wears old-man slippers in a dingy Greenwich Village comedy club. Jack Daniel's fits in everywhere.

Jack Daniel's doesn't call itself bourbon, although technically it could be called exactly that because it follows those same rules for bourbon making. What sets Jack Daniel's apart is that it goes through a step called the "Lincoln County process," which involves dripping new spirit through sugar maple charcoal before putting it in wood. Tennessee distillers like Jack Daniel's and George Dickel who use the Lincoln County process claim that the filtering both mellows and imparts a sugary maple element to the overall whiskey character. As of May 2013, any brand in Tennessee (where Jack Daniel's is made) that wants to label itself a Tennessee whiskey must now use the Lincoln County process.

## The Jack Daniel's Label Says "Sour Mash." What Does That Mean?

The answer is short and sweet: Sour mash whiskey does not refer to a sour flavor or any kind of special sour mash flavor; it simply refers to the practice of adding a bit of mash from older "runs" to the current mash. The addition of already-fermented mash ensures consistency from batch to batch, controls pH levels so that yeast can do its sugar-eating job most effectively, and inhibits bacterial growth. Most whiskeys use the sour mash process.

I do not include Jack Daniel's Tennessee Whiskey in my recommended tastings in this book because: first, it stands out there on its own anyway, proud in its dramatically different flavor, and second, I wager that there are only one or two of you reading this who haven't already tried it in Coke or out of a plastic Crush bottle behind the neighborhood scalawag's house in the ninth grade.

### SOUR MASH IS NOW MARKETED TO MEAN . . .

The down-home feel of the phrase "sour mash" conjures up images of bad boys making whiskey in the backwoods of the Tennessee mountains. You might think "salt of the earth" and "authentic," and that's the reason why you'll see the words "sour mash" written across many bottles these days. Brands want to capture that old-timey feeling, to offer you a keyhole peek into a sepia-toned southern American fantasy through your drink.

## IRISH WHISKEY

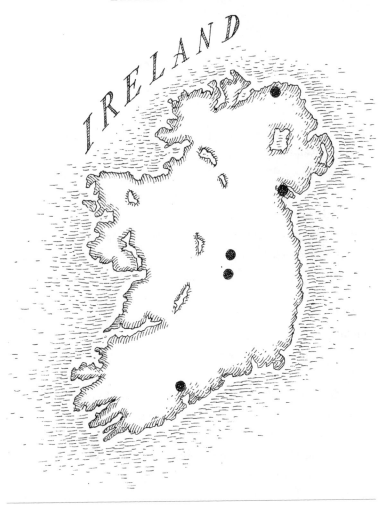

*Ireland's distilleries dwindled over the past two centuries, but promise to come back with a vengeance. The northernmost distillery is Bushmill's and the southernmost distillery is Middleton's, home to Jameson Irish Whiskey.*

*Pot Still, Grain, Single Malt and Blended,*
*The bouquet of fine flavors in front of me ended*
*Lightly Kerschnickered*
*Then properly liquored*
*That whiskey? I'd sure recommend it!*

THE AUTHOR

Independence from England in the 1800s, a failure to adopt column stills, and America's Prohibition drove Irish whiskey virtually out of business. Here's how that happened: The English stopped drinking Irish whiskey, Scotland churned out big quantities of whisky in the column still and dropped prices, and America shut its doors to liquor altogether. By the 1960s only 1 percent of whiskey drinkers were enjoying Ireland's holy spirit, a terrible fate for a country so entrenched in whiskey history.

Thank God, then, we have people like Tim Herlihy, whiskey ambassador to Irish brand Tullamore Dew, to get us all back on track. Tim is my Irish superhero: the unassuming son of an egg farmer from northern Dublin plucked from obscurity and placed in Gotham to save us all from our Irish-whiskey ignorance.

I met Tim years ago in Ireland before his big move to New York, and I liked him right away. He nodded his head when I told him I thought Tullamore Dew, his brand, smelled like the fresh math paper I remember smelling in second grade. He was patient with me in the car as we drove around Dublin and I peppered him with Irish whiskey and egg questions, two rather rusty topics for me at the time: "What's the difference between brown and white eggs?" *Nothing, except for color it turns out.* "How many chickens on your farm?" *Chickens don't lay eggs. Hens do. Thousands.* "How many distilleries operate in Ireland?" *Just three right now: Midleton, Old Bushmills, and Cooley. All Irish brands like Jameson and Bushmills are made by one of those.* "Is all Irish whiskey triple distilled?" *No, not at all. That's a myth.* Finally, as the only egg farmer cum whiskey ambassador in the world, this makes Tim the authority on hangover egg sandwiches, too. "What's the best whiskey hangover cure?" *A brekkie roll, the Irish destruction of the French baguette, loaded up with fried eggs, bacon, AND sausage* (aka the "I had a night out with Tully Tim" antidote).

"Tully Tim" helped me rethink Irish whiskey (and eggs), which I'd rejected out of hand for a long time, partly because I'd grown up around too many guys named Sully pounding shots, and partly because I would reject anything my family thought was totally awesome—oi-rish *anything*. But you know what? Jameson on ice in a keg cup is pretty good. It works here. And beyond that, Irish whiskey can be elegant, subtle, and downright delicious.

### Irish Whiskey Styles

Jameson and Tullamore Dew are examples of Irish blends. They are produced using a combination of three different distillates, which is essentially what we call a mash bill in America:

Single malt, made with 100 percent malted barley
Grain whiskey, made predominantly with corn
Pot still, made with a combination of unmalted and
malted barley, the only of its kind in the whiskey world

Here's how to put together Irish whiskey combinations. Most well-known Irish whiskey brands are a combination of those three components. For example:

Grain + Pot still = Jameson and Powers
Grain + Malt = Bushmills and Kilbeggan
Pot still + Malt = The Irishman and Writers Tears (rare styles
in the United States)
Grain + Malt + Pot still = Tullamore Dew Blend

Easy, right? Two types of distillate come together to make the blends. But Irish whiskey doesn't stop there. Each of those Irish whiskey blend "distillates" has an affiliated brand for you to try as well. Below I list in more detail the ones you can find beyond the Emerald Isle.

## SINGLE GRAIN WHISKEY

Single grain whiskeys from Ireland are found mostly in blends. But one of the big three Irish distillers, Cooley, bottles a pure single grain in a brand called Glenore. It is double distilled and matured in refill bourbon casks from the United States, the way most Scotch is.

The 95 percent corn content makes this whiskey a true standout: Bourbon lovers will recognize the familiar corn sweetness, but those looking for the refinement of an aged whiskey will find that, too—Glenore is bottled at eight and fifteen years old and sold worldwide.

### Irish Pure Pot Still

Clever whiskey makers looking to evade taxes on malted barley got smart and said, "Oh yeah? Throw some unmalted barley in that goddamned mash then," and hence pure pot still was born. It's a style of whiskey unique to Ireland, born out of a feisty spirit and subversiveness.

Pure pot still is a sublime and silky, mouthwatering Irish whiskey, aged perfectly in warehouses south of Cork where Midleton, the world's only pure pot still distiller, makes it. Two brands I love are called Redbreast and Green Spot. Don't be confused here—the Irish whiskey world functions a bit like the American landscape, one distillery can make many brands and styles: Midleton also makes Jameson and a myriad of other styles under names such as Tullamore Dew and Powers. (Tullamore Dew is now building a sparkling new distillery in the heart of Ireland and will be making its own whiskey soon.) Midleton grows its own barley, uses fresh local spring water, and has perfected the art of cask aging that makes pure pot stills like Redbreast and Green Spot taste so good. I've turned on loads of people to Irish whiskey by serving up a dram of Redbreast 15, which comes out in limited quantities and has all the premium qualities of complexity and flavor you'd find in a Scotch.

### Irish Single Malt

Miss Colleen was a beauty pageant held every year in Holyoke, Massachusetts, near where I grew up. Winning the Miss Colleen pageant was considered the epitome of success and glamour for the Irish American girls in my area. The St. Patrick's Day Parade, where Miss Colleen was announced and paraded in front of Irish revelers sitting on plastic folding chairs and drinking out of lunch bags, remains one of the biggest parades in the country. I wanted to be like all those other Irish American kids around town, and once even asked why I couldn't go to CCD— Confraternity of Christian Doctrine—on Wednesday afternoons, like the lot of them. "You are not Catholic," my mother would remind me. Ironically, she went to Catholic schools until she was eighteen. But that's a story for another book.

I remember clearly that the Irish whiskey brand Bushmills was taboo in certain crowds when I was growing up—it was a Northern Ireland whiskey, the "Protestant whiskey" some snickered. Besides secular Jack Daniel's, my first taste of Irish whiskey must have been Jameson, but I don't actually remember. Does religious-affiliated whiskey sound nuts? I think so, too. Imagine my surprise, then, when many years later during a whiskey tasting class in Philadelphia someone got very angry with me for drinking Bushmills. "A betrayal," he called it.

Founded in 1608, Bushmills is the oldest licensed operating distillery in the world. What I like about Bushmills is that the narrowness of their style has allowed them to really hone and focus on what they do best: aged single malts, double distilled, with an attention to carefully chosen casks from all over the world. They do make a blend (traditional

Bushmills), but if you want to capture the beauty of an Irish whiskey beyond the shot culture, taste the Bushmills 16 single malt, which is aged in old bourbon casks and oloroso sherry casks for sixteen years, then married together in a port-seasoned cask before bottling.

Bushmills has carried the single malt torch for Irish whiskey, churning out fine whiskey for hundreds of years and preparing our palates for the recent Irish single malt resurgence on the American market. Tullamore Dew 10, The Tyrconnell, and the only Irish peated whiskey brand, Connemara, all export Irish single malts worldwide. I recommend any of them for a home tasting, or highly suggest you give them a try at your local bar. The Tyrconnell and Connemara are both produced at the Cooley Distillery, while Tullamore Dew is produced at Midleton to the south, until their new distillery is finished.

I didn't list any production rules for Irish whiskey up front because there aren't that many: It must be distilled in Ireland (no surprise), aged in wood casks for three years (no mention of cask type), and take on some flavor of the cereals in the distillate (what whiskey doesn't?). In fact, the Irish Whiskey Act hasn't been updated since it was created in 1980 with vague definitions as to what a distiller can bottle—no reference to Irish single malt or to Irish single grain whiskey was even included. The upside is that the lack of rules make the Irish whiskey frontier exciting, with new distilleries and brands popping up in Ireland regularly. And with Irish whiskey's tremendous 400 percent growth since 2002, I don't imagine strict rules coming down the pike anytime soon.

In the meantime, look out for Tully Tim in your town. He flies all over the United States looking to rescue you, too, from your Irish whiskey prejudices. On our last night together, Tim bought a dram of Tullamore Dew 10 for everyone sitting around us and passionately explained its charm: First, the single malt is triple distilled and aged in a seasoned bourbon barrel from the United States. After ten years, the contents of the barrel is divvied up and placed in Madeira, port, and sherry casks, aged anywhere from three to six months, and then reunited in a vat to intermingle before bottling.

This sort of precision and creativity is what makes the future of Irish whiskey so exciting to us whiskey geeks.

Irish Single Malt Focus Flight
Tullamore Dew 10
Bushmills 16
Knappogue Castle 12
The Tyrconnell
Connemara Peated

Swap in a Few of These with the Single Malts to
Create an "Irish Whiskey Sampler" Flight
Greenore Irish Grain 8
Redbreast Pure Pot Still 15
Green Spot Pure Pot Still
Bushmills Blended Original
Jameson 18 Blended

Finally, before you toast your good fortune at rediscovering Irish whiskey, here's a little prayer:

*Our Whiskey*
*Which art in Barrels*
*Hallowed be thy drink*
*They will be drunk*
*I will be drunk*
*At home as in the tavern*
*Give us this day our daily spirit*
*And forgive us our livers!*

*Forgive us our spillages*
*As we forgive those who spillage against us*
*Save us from hangovers,*
*For thine is whiskey—the HOLY SPIRITS*
*The triple distilled, the triple blended*
*For ever and ever.*

TULLAMORE TIM HERLIHY

## JAPANESE WHISKY

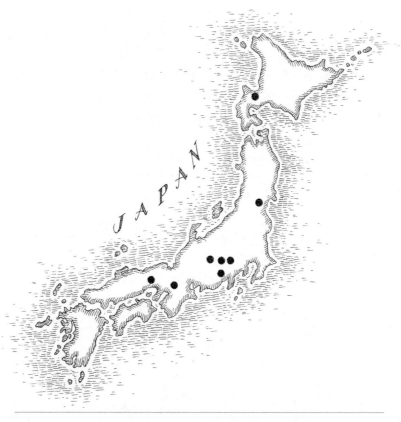

Nikka and Suntory dominate the whisky landscape in Japan with
distilleries that operate as far north as the island of Hokkaido and as far south as Kyoto.
The Japanese have been making whisky since the 1920s.

After the long twenty-hour journey from New York to Tokyo, I rewarded myself with a dash into a Japanese convenience store called Lawson to pick up some fine sushi, whisky, and chopsticks. I held a royal Japanese picnic in the hotel room before nodding off into a deep sleep. Inevitably, I woke up jet-lagged and too early. I dug out some of the Lawson nori that I had crammed into the hotel minibar the night before and enjoyed a breakfast of hotel espresso and more corner-store cuisine. If this all sounds weird to you, allow me to let you in on the secret: Lawson is pretty darn good. I once heard David Chang, renowned chef and founder of Momofuku, announce that he could eat all his meals there. See? David Chang said it. On national TV. Wipe that smirk off your face! A Japanese culinary adventure, it only goes uphill from there.

The Japanese seem to do everything just a little bit better than everyone else—they have an attention to detail and pride in any task, no matter how mundane, that separates their character from the rest of our sorry lot. Convenience-store food there is about as good as food in a few sit-down restaurants in New York. And those preparing the food obviously take it very seriously. Store clerks spent twenty minutes wrapping my souvenirs with crispy cellophane and ribbon, and then they stickered and stamped the gift bags as if they were performing a tea ceremony for a queen. Even cab drivers wore white gloves. Bento boxes—train station fast food—were neatly compartmentalized into little sections and wrapped into brightly decorated boxes that looked like children's birthday gifts.

The philosophy of whisky making that informs Japanese distillers mirrors the ideology of the culture as a whole, and can be summed up in two words: *continuous refinement*. It means that the Japanese are always testing and refining their processes to see if they can improve on taste and flavor. Over time—maybe ten years or so—you might taste a difference between two Yamazaki 12 expressions. From year to year, however, those subtle differences go largely unnoticed. This is an important distinction from Scotch. In Scotland, holding on to tradition is what dictates the underlying approach to whisky making. Under no circumstances would the makers of GlenDronach 12 want it to change over time, so trying out a new pot still size or playing with a yeast strain to tweak a character note are not the kinds of things the Scottish tend to do.

But playing and refining pays off for the Japanese. I don't say this lightly: I haven't yet met a Japanese whisky that I didn't enjoy. I struggle to find words to describe Japanese whisky, so instead I offer this: The Japanese *totally* nail it. So few big companies operate in Japan that each one needs to be 100 percent self-reliant—an enclosed, self-sustaining system that can churn out robust and vibrant whisky fit for a fickle and refined Japanese palate. While Japanese whisky companies like Suntory also use barley as the predominant grain and the same style of stills the Scottish use, they require six different pot still shapes all used in an endless combination to fine-tune flavor for the variants they bottle. In Scotland, most distilleries, you will remember, have their own signature stills—maybe two or three variations at most.

The two Suntory distilleries, Yamazaki and Hakushu, also mingle casks to create a blend called Hibiki. But they'll neither trade nor out-source with other Japanese whisky companies the way the Scotch, Irish, and American whiskeys might. In fact, the only other major whisky pro-ducer in Japan—Nikka—is a most unlikely candidate to begin any sort of friendly trading with Suntory. Their founders, Shinjiro Torii and Ma-sataka Taketsuru, were once business partners.

The original intent when Shinjiro Torii and his distillery executive Masataka Taketsuru exploded onto the Japanese spirit scene in 1924 was to bring a food-friendly, Scotch-style whisky to the Japanese masses. They built pot stills less than a half mile from the birthplace of the Japanese tea ceremony, a sacred and misty little place outside of Kyoto, where water from numerous streams and rivers meet at the foot of bamboo-covered hills. Years would pass before they released a too-peated whisky. A full decade passed before Suntory produced something drinkable in 1937. Taketsuru was already gone by then. The Scotland-trained distillery executive working under Torii left to create Nikka in 1934, leaving Torii and his start-up, Suntory, to expand on their own. Both distilleries have been on fire ever since.

Let's run through the distilleries and available brands operating under the two companies—there aren't too many of them, and any of them you can get your hands on will be a nice addition to a good whisky collection, or a great dram to try in a restaurant with some wagyu beef or fresh sashimi, of course.

### SUNTORY
Yamazaki Distillery—12, 18, 25 single malts
Hakushu Distillery—12, 17 single malt
Hibiki—blend of Yamazaki and Hakushu single malts + grain whisky

### NIKKA DISTILLERIES
Yoichi 15 single malt
Miyagikyo 12 single malt
Nikka Taketsuru 17 pure malt—blend of malts from
Yoichi and Miyagiko
Nikka Taketsuru 12 pure malt—blend of malts from
Yoichi and Miyagiko
Nikka Coffey Grain—grain whisky made in Coffey stills
(see Column Stills, chapter 2)

## Nosing and Tasting Japanese Whisky

Japanese whiskies are exciting to nose and taste. The Yamazaki expressions delivered a silky mouthfeel of tropical fruit notes like pineapple. But notice there's something else unique in there, too—a nuanced soft and spicy floral. You'll know it when you nose it. This exotic aromatic evokes the slight incense haze surrounding Buddhist temples, and comes from the Mizunara cask, made from Japanese oak. Taste a Hakushu 12 against a traditional Islay Scotch expression—the smoky and peaty note of the Hakushu 12 won't bonk you on the head with a sledgehammer the way some of the Islay malts do. Rather, it's a subtle, friendly note that only reminds you of its distant Scotch cousin. Or, as some say, siblings separated at birth. Nikka whisky such as the Taketsuru pure malt lingers on the back palate with spice, chocolate, sweet smoke, and coffee in the most gentle manner, a testament to the accuracy with which Nikka matures slightly peated barley in seasoned casks.

## THE JAPANESE HIGHBALL

### RECIPE FOR A TRUE WHISKY-LOVING GEEK

Try this crisp and refreshing elixir at home, inspired by bars in Tokyo that have raised a simple concoction of whisky, ice, and soda water to a high art form. A Japanese highball isn't like the soda water from a gun you've had over crushed ice in a pint glass. *Au contraire.* It honors the Japanese reverence for water. This at-home recipe uses similar freezing techniques and a good sparkling water accompaniment to enhance the whisky without any dilution. Here's how to do it:

### ICE

The trick is to start with the clearest, most beautiful gem of an ice cube possible. In Japan they have special equipment that slowly freezes ice, removing any impurities (like bubbles) that make the ice cloudy. You can re-create this at home by either setting your freezer thermostat at 30 degrees or the highest shelf of your refrigerator at the same. After twenty-four hours you should have a pretty nice cube—at least less cloudy and weak than you normally might. Slowly frozen ice will last longer in your cocktail.

## SODA

Choose a sparkling water with small bubbles and low saltiness or mineral content. I like San Pellegrino as well as Badoit. Lighter effervescence creates a softer cocktail.

## WHISKY

Freeze your highball bottles. For a slightly peated highball, the Hakushu 12 is lovely. Otherwise, experiment with any of the Japanese whiskies available to you.

## GLASSWARE

Use a tall, slender glass—a Collins glass is best. First add your whisky, layer in the ice, and finally the water—carefully pour down the side of the glass on the sides of the cube, a ritual performed at the Star Bar Ginza in Tokyo. Highball master Hisashi Kishi claims that this technique results in the best overall texture. I can't argue. It is delicious.

Winston Churchill was known to enjoy a highball or two. On a 1954 flight, according to *The Telegraph*, for breakfast he ordered a poached egg, toast, jam, butter, coffee with milk, a jug of cold milk, cold chicken or meat. On his second tray: grapefruit, sugar bowl, glass of orange juice, whisky, and soda water. Apparently, he and President Truman had breakfast preferences in common (see the bourbon section in this chapter).

## Canadian Whisky

In 2009, I needed to sneak a couple cases of Scotch into New York from Scotland. I had collected them while working at the Scotch Malt Whisky Society in Edinburgh, and some of the bottles came from distilleries that don't even operate anymore. So I decided to book a ticket on a cruise ship because I knew the porters would carry on board whatever you could fit into your room, no questions asked. My husband and I discovered that toward the end of summer, some of the cruise ships that tool around Europe during July and August "reposition" to the Caribbean for the long winters that start in September, and tickets on one of those repositioning cruises are cheap. The disadvantage was that it meant making more than ten port stops along the way: England, France, Ireland, and Canada. It was an awful trip. We hit terrible weather, ten-foot surges, and longed for the mangy port-town pubs, which were scheduled every couple of days so we could find our land legs. We spent a lot of time in bed, but when we managed to amble around the ship, we witnessed hot dog and Coke vomit decorating the poolside rather than beach towels and beer bottles. One good thing did happen on that trip, though: I discovered the deep and quiet beauty of Nova Scotia ("New Scotland") and the taste of North America's first single malt whisky, Glen Breton, bottled by Glenora Distillery. It's a good little whisky, produced in a single malt Scotch style using barley and pot stills, releasing florals, fruits, slight spice, and mild vanillas.

Glenora is one of the first of the microdistillery movement under way in Canada, with a half dozen located right in or around Nova Scotia. Unfortunately, you'll be hard pressed to find many small-batch Canadian-style whiskies around the United States . . . yet. You'll pay almost $100 for a bottle of Glen Breton when you do. Canadianwhisky.org lists dozens of small distillers opening in Canada in what they call "leaps and bounds," complete with an interactive map to indicate where the latest microdistillers are located. For now, most of you will have to choose between brands like Canadian Club and Crown Royal, whiskies made primarily with corn and other grains and produced in large enough quantities to make them two of the biggest whiskey brands in the world. These whiskies are very light and best served on the rocks.

Distilleries in Canada, which once numbered in the hundreds, have dwindled into a somewhat passionless industry of less than a dozen big blended whisky producers focused on output of tremendous scale. This doesn't necessarily mean that you can't find a tasty Canadian whisky; rather, the discussion often becomes a blander one consisting of which rich industrialist bought which big distillery and made it even bigger during the latter half of the twentieth century. The Canadian whisky conversation is kind of like reading about mergers and acquisitions in *The Wall Street Journal*—interesting in a way, but not very sexy. Davin de Kergommeaux gets into the discussion best in his Canadian whisky history, *Canadian Whisky: The Portable Expert*, if you are hungry for some serious discussion on all those consolidations, Canadian whisky families, and some distillery history.

Although Canadians interchange the words "rye" and "whisky," most whiskey produced and sold in Canada has little, if any, rye content. This is a holdover name given to Canadian whisky that at one time would have included actual rye in the production. WhistlePig, an American whiskey company based in Vermont, actually buys Canadian casks filled with aged rye spirit to bottle and sell. It's a delicious whiskey—a peek into some of the whiskey treasures that must be hiding north of the border. I hope it's also a precursor of good things to come.

## WHISKEY IN THE REST OF THE WORLD

My tongue cracked and burned for two days after I sat on a blind tasting speed panel with five New York whiskey retailers and restaurateurs to evaluate whiskeys. We tasted ninety-two whiskeys in about eight hours. Yes, of course I spit them out after tasting. And no, I don't recommend trying that at home. My palate became fatigued, my nose stopped detecting anything interesting, and I wondered why on earth these sorts of awards panels exist anyway. I made my way to the end, revisited a few that confused me, and powered through the burn. All for you.

An interesting pattern emerged, and for that I'm thankful for the whiskey marathon. In a sea of whiskeys, those that stood out came from the nonproducing whiskey nations, places like South America, France, and Taiwan. Something about these whiskeys excited our palates and provided the much-needed departure from a taste profile beyond "Yeah, that tastes like another Scotch to me." And the best part? None of these whiskeys broke the bank. Let me share with you some of my favorite whiskeys that come from regions outside of the biggies, and why I like them. And when you see a new whiskey from a country that doesn't normally produce whiskey, don't be afraid—give it a try!

## South Africa

Three Ships whisky from Wellington, South Africa, makes a peated and smoked Scotch whisky–style expression called "5 Year Old Premium Select." It is a gutsy move in an industry that normally shies away from making a whiskey that young. While it is not sold by U.S. retailers just yet, I include it because it is winning so many international whiskey awards, and I'm banking on its coming to the United States soon. In the meantime, get a traveling friend to snag you a bottle from a duty-free shop when they travel abroad. The Three Ships Bourbon Cask Finish, made from a blend of grains and malts, displays a golden, sweet, and lush palate—it was one of my favorite whiskeys among those I tasted during a recent whiskey competition in New York. Three Ships has been around for a long time, too. Founded in 1886, the distillery, James Sedgwick, has been quietly churning out whiskey for a half century, af-

Manhattan

Whiskey Sour

Blood and Sand

Egg White Sour

37 West 26 Street

Scottish Chai

Kilimanjaro

Addie Graham

Autumn Poet

Lime Thyme
Sour

Tendril

Pathak's Punch

Canadian Sneak

Green Glory Fizz

French Connection

Fool's Gold

Old-Fashioned

Mint Juleps

ter trying its hand at brandies and grape juice. I'm glad it moved beyond the sippy cup set.

And be sure to check out one of the best single grain whiskeys available anywhere—Bain's Cape Mountain—a well-rounded and approachable grain whiskey also produced at the same distillery. Whether you sip it neat, blend it into a cocktail, or throw it over ice with an orange peel, I think it might very well be the antidote to a rough day.

## France

While South Africa is putting out whiskeys in a Scotch style—and even perfecting the flavor at a better price—the new French whiskeys demonstrate terroir better than any whiskey I can think of, making it difficult to relate French whiskeys to any other country's whiskey. Brenne, a French whiskey made with barley that grows alongside grapes used for producing cognac and is aged in old cognac casks, tastes remarkably, well . . . *French*. It's elegant and fruity, with a slight tropical banana note that I've never tasted in any whiskey. It sits between a cognac (distilled from grapes) and whiskey. I tell people new to whiskey to taste whiskeys like Brenne and to try not to compare it with Scotch whisky or bourbon. Brenne is totally unique, unencumbered by competitors or preconceived notions of what a French whiskey should taste like. (In fact, I like it so much that I've included a recipe using Brenne in the original cocktail section in chapter 5.) If you can't find Brenne—it sells out fast—try the Bastille brand, which carries some aromatics (not all) similar to those of Brenne.

## Sweden

Did you forget to do something totally cool in college, like build a multibillion-dollar social media site, or say, a distillery? Yeah, me, too, although I did manage to make a professional career out of drinking.

For a group of Swedish university students with a bright idea, whiskey love, and some smarts to boot, a party ski weekend led to the creation of Mackmyra, Sweden's first whiskey that is made with an "elegant recipe," a vague description that both frustrates me and makes me laugh. I have no idea what it is.

In any event, that "elegant recipe" is matured mostly in first-fill Swedish "roasted" oak barrels and the result is a gorgeous medley of mint, caramel, spice, vanilla, and a tinge of juniper, which is lit and imparted into the grain somewhere along the line. I expect this brand to be around for a while and to expand, but I'm also confident that the variants and styles and maybe even that secret recipe will change. If you see a bottle, it's a good bet and worth a try.


## India

When I lived in Edinburgh as my base for touring Europe with my band, I tried to do a couple of gigs and radio spots locally in town. I would call and the producer or booker would invariably ask, "Where do you live, and when are you coming to town?" I'd answer, "I've lived here for a year or so!" He'd hang up. On the other hand, when I called these same places from down the street and said, "I'm from New York, I'll be in town in a couple of months," the response would be, "Great! Let's do it." It was as if Edinburgh couldn't believe that anyone worthwhile could live there and be a good musician—a form of self-hatred, I think. So what does this have to do with Indian whiskey, you wonder?

India doesn't stock its own homegrown and award-winning whiskey. Anywhere. On back bars, in resorts, tourist centers, or big cities, you'll find only the big Scotch companies like Johnnie Walker, Glenfiddich, and The Macallan. This seriously mystified me during my travels there. While I did find out that it's a pay-to-play market, that is, a company must pay the state in order to be made available, most people there snickered when I'd talk about my favorite Indian whiskey brand, Amrut Fusion. The company, which has been around for more than fifty years, decided to focus Amrut sales in Scotland rather than India, and supplied their own country of more than a billion people with a mere one thousand cases. For many burgeoning whiskey companies from around the world, the idea of a head-to-head challenge with the Scotch marketplace is just too enticing to turn down. I actually first tasted Amrut in New Jersey, rather than in Mumbai and New Delhi.

Amrut Fusion, Amrut's slightly peated bottling, has won numerous accolades and awards in blind tastings. As the Japanese do, Amrut takes the peat and smoke elements that the Islay Scotches do very well and tames them. Whenever I reveal a favorite whiskey to be an Indian one in a blind tasting lineup, somebody inevitably gasps in disbelief. But it shouldn't come as a surprise that India is a whiskey player—Indians certainly have a long history of getting a balance of spices and nuance right in their cuisine.

### And More . . .

Truth be told, I could write a second book on the latest whiskeys being created around the world. Taiwan's Kavalan range got my palate very excited during my marathon tasting, and even little old Tasmania is exporting something other than a whirling cartoon character. I just received "Batch Number One" of a New Zealand whiskey as a gift from a friend who snuck it into her suitcase for me. It's finished in New Zealand red wine casks. My point here is to make sure you understand not to overlook whiskeys that come from places outside America, Scotland, and Ireland. And when you see them offered at a bar, ask your bartender what the profile of the whiskey is and see if it fits the sort of profile you normally like.

## TABLE 3: YOUR WHISKEY CONVERSATION (OR REBUTTAL) CHART

| THE TOPIC | SNAPSHOT FACTS | THE MYTHS | THE REBUTTAL |
|---|---|---|---|
| Scotch, Single Malt (SMS) | Mash is 100% malted barley.<br><br>Matured in Scotland<br><br>Oak casks only, minimum of 3 years<br><br>Pot-still distilled<br><br>Bottled at 40% ABV<br><br>From one distillery only | Ice not allowed.<br><br><br>Older is better.<br><br><br><br><br>All Scotch is peated/smoky.<br><br>Never in cocktails<br><br><br><br><br><br><br>The Brand X is the best! | Ice mitigates or permits different flavors. Even top distillers drink with ice.<br><br>Younger whiskies are very fresh, with elements of distillation and fermentation shining through.<br><br>Roughly 10% are peated/smoky. The rest are 70% cask-aged influenced.<br><br>An SMS with its myriad aromatic properties and notes can make a delicious, complex cocktail in the right hands.<br><br>There are more than 100 SMS brands to choose from. Don't limit yourself to only one brand. Taste is subjective! |
| Scotch, Blend | Made with a blend of grains and malt distilleries in one bottle<br><br>Continuous distillation (column stills)<br><br>Aged in oak casks, minimum of 3 years<br><br>Bottled at 40% ABV | Blended whiskies are of a lesser quality than single malts.<br><br>Johnnie Walker Blue must not be a blend, because it's so expensive.<br><br>They are all peated/smoky. | There is an art to blending. When done right, can create a premium-quality whisky.<br><br>Johnnie Walker Blue is a blend, no matter what the price your boss paid.<br><br>Blends are often peated/smoky, but not always. Islay whiskies are often a blend component. |

| THE TOPIC | SNAPSHOT FACTS | THE MYTHS | THE REBUTTAL |
|---|---|---|---|
| Scotch, Blended Malt | Blend of different single malt Scotches<br><br>Matured in Scotland<br><br>Bottled at minimum 40% ABV | A blended malt Scotch is the same as a blended Scotch. | A blended malt is a blend of single malts; therefore it is made with 100% barley. A blended Scotch is a blend of Scotch grain whisky and single malts. Blended malt Scotches used to be called vatted or pure malts. |
| Irish Whiskey | Irish whiskey styles are pot still, grain single malt, and blend. Styles are made with different grains and distilled in different still types: pot and column.<br><br>Only three big players in the game right now, making most of the available brands.<br><br>Pot still whiskey in Ireland refers to the use of malted and unmalted barley, in addition to the pot still used. It is the only place in the world to make it. | There are Protestant whiskeys and Catholic ones.<br><br>Irish whiskey is for shots.<br><br>Ireland is the motherland of whiskey.<br><br>All Irish whiskeys are triple distilled.<br><br>No peated/smoky whiskeys are made in Ireland, only Scotland. | Only in America. No one talks about that in Ireland. Religion doesn't belong in my drink choice.<br><br>Many Irish whiskeys are luxurious. Get over the Irish-shot image and try Redbreast 15.<br><br>Sadly, no. That crown still belongs to Scotland.<br><br>Some Irish whiskeys are triple distilled, some are not.<br><br>Connemara is a peated whiskey. Not all Scotch is peated, either. |

| THE TOPIC | SNAPSHOT FACTS | THE MYTHS | THE REBUTTAL |
|---|---|---|---|
| American, Bourbon | Made with at least 51% corn in the mash bill<br><br>Aged in charred, new oak barrels<br><br>Put into casks at a minimum of 100 proof<br><br>Bottled at a minimum of 80 proof<br><br>Pot stills or column stills can be used, or both. | Bourbon can be made in Kentucky only. | Bourbon can be made anywhere in the U.S.A. |
| | | Bourbon began in Kentucky. | We don't know exactly where bourbon was born. |
| | | Bourbon is less premium than Scotch. | Bourbon is a different style of whiskey, with many luxurious and premium styles that match the beauty of a Scotch. |
| | | Older is better. | Bourbon can become too woody as it gets older. It doesn't need that long in a cask. |
| | | Pappy Van Winkle is the best! | Taste is subjective; Pappy is good, but may not be the best. Depends on your palate. |
| American, Rye | Made with at least 51% rye in mash bill<br><br>Aged in charred, new oak barrels<br><br>Put into casks at 100 proof<br><br>Bottled at a minimum of 80 proof<br><br>Generally spicier (more peppery) and drier than bourbon | It's not as good as bourbon. | Taste is subjective. You might love rye. I do. It's spicy and offers a nice bitterness. |
| American, Single Malt | Made with at least 51% malted barley in mash bill<br><br>Aged in charred, new oak barrels<br><br>Put into casks at 100 proof<br><br>Bottled at a minimum of 80 proof | America makes single malts? | Hell yeah it does! Try Balcones, Pine Barrens, Corsair, McCarthy's, Hudson. |
| | | American single malt is not as good as SMS. | American single malts win medals and beat out Scotches in tasting competitions. |

| THE TOPIC | SNAPSHOT FACTS | THE MYTHS | THE REBUTTAL |
|---|---|---|---|
| American, Corn Whiskey | Made with 80% corn<br><br>Can be aged in used or uncharred barrels<br><br>Put into casks at 100 proof<br><br>Bottled at a minimum of 80 proof | Corn is corn.<br><br><br><br><br>Corn is boring. | Check out the Balcones and Hudson range, which play with corn varietals. Popcorn tastes different from corn on the cob, no?<br><br>Corn is uniquely American, and the varieties can impart different flavors. |
| American, Moonshine/ White Whiskey | "Moonshine" is a term to describe illegally made whiskey.<br><br>White whiskey is generally unaged bourbon, rye, or American single malt; whatever is being made for aging at a distillery is often bottled early for white whiskey.<br><br>"White whiskey," "moonshine," "white dog," "white lighting" are words that people interchange, even on labels.<br><br>White whiskey can be made with any grain in any still.<br><br>Most white whiskeys will tell you what's in the bottle, whether that's corn, rye, malt, or a blend. | It says "moonshine," so it is.<br><br><br><br><br><br>White whiskies don't taste good. | A label that uses the term "moonshine" is doing so for fun and to catch your eye, even though it might be made exactly like a moonshiner might have made it.<br><br>Most people prefer whiskey aged in wood, but white whiskey can be fun, add variety to your whiskey closet, make great cocktails, and demonstrate grain character unmasked by wood. When you buy it, you may be helping to support your local distiller until it is up and running with aged hooch. |
| Japanese, Single Malt | Made in the Scotch style (barley, various seasoned oak)<br><br>Often uses special Japanese casks called Mizunara | The Japanese make whiskey? | The Japanese have been making whiskey for close to 100 years. Their expressions are in high demand for their lush beauty and subtleties. |

| THE TOPIC | SNAPSHOT FACTS | THE MYTHS | THE REBUTTAL |
|---|---|---|---|
| Canadian Whisky | New distilleries popping up; keep an eye out for innovation as the scene grows. Very vague definitions of what makes Canadian whisky Canadian. | Canadian whisky made with rye | "Rye" and "whisky" are interchangeable terms in Canada, although very few of the whiskies you'll taste contain very much rye anymore. Look out for some of the new whiskies on the horizon, though. |
| Craft Whiskey | No universal definition of the word "craft" exists. | Craft is better. | Some craft whiskeys are great, but they are not universally better than large whiskey distiller products. |
| | | Craft means small. | Some large producers are creating "craft" lines of whiskeys. |
| | | Craft means they do everything on-site. | Some "craft" distillers outsource the distillate or even finished product. |

# 4

## Building Your Bar and Your Confidence

*Starter Collection Tips, Glassware, and More*

### THE WHISKEY CLOSET

Now you have a sense of your palate preferences. Maybe you've discovered you are thirsty for whisky from Scotland or Japan. Next step? Build a killer home whiskey collection that will reflect your unique tastes and interests, budget, and how you entertain at home. My own collection began ten years ago with a heavy emphasis on nonpeated single malt Scotch. I was living in Scotland and had access to some pretty phenomenal options at a reasonable price, but I wasn't flush with cash, so unless I was absolutely sure it would please my palate every time I poured a dram, I didn't buy it. I couldn't afford the risk. In this chapter, I'll teach you a couple of tricks to minimize "bottle purchase regret," from free ways to sample whiskey to advice on making a best-guess about whether or not you'll like a bottle, even if you haven't tried it.

When I started collecting whiskey, I bought about one bottle per month, never spending more than around $50. After a year, I had a tiny but very nice Scotch whisky collection that I proudly displayed on an old marble mantel, next to my piano. Every bottle was a reflection of my own personal choice, and I'd learned everything I could about it. I could tell my guests why I'd bought it, and what's more I could tell them why I served a particular bottle to *them*.

My collection has grown since then, and now includes a full spectrum of whiskeys from around the world—some of my favorite ones aren't even full bottles. I cherish a special 5-ounce sample of the first rye off the stills at Kings County Distillery in Brooklyn, given to me for my birthday, with "Magic Awesome" written in black Sharpie across the front. I'm not fussed about packaging.

I don't believe you need to invest heavily in whiskeys to start building a solid collection. I didn't. And if you have access to a store that sells a variety of American whiskeys, even better, as you can start your whiskey collection by buying bottles for less than $40. That said, as the demand continues to rise for all things whiskey, so do prices across all styles—American whiskey included. More than ever, it is important for you to familiarize yourself with your own palate and have the ability to navigate labels so that you know exactly what you're buying. As always, check your age statements, "distilled by" designations, and other signifiers such as region and substyle within that region. And remember that the distillery marketing team's job is to woo you with fabulous stories and packaging, too. So, make sure you take all the messaging with a grain of salt. Your palate and wallet trump all.

I recommend that you start your collection with options that pair well with food, make delicious cocktails, and can be served both neat and on the rocks. I keep my recommendations for American whiskey below $40 and $60 for Irish, Scotch, and artisanal distillers. You can start a solid collection with bottles at those prices. After that? Sky's the limit.

## "CONTROL STATES" VERSUS "FREE STATES"

### How Whiskey Gets to Your Restaurant or Store

You might be reading this book in what we in the industry call a "control state." A control state is a state (there are currently eighteen of them) in which a government bureau sets prices of brands and decides which brands will be for sale in the state-run stores. This means that finding a certain brand or vintage can become a daunting task when your state's bureau decides not to stock it. If you are a bar owner in one of the control states, you know this system well: Every week you might visit your state-run store to buy your alcohol. If you are what's called a *supplier* (distiller, big liquor company), once or twice a year you'll visit the state government offices to try to make sure the state carries your product.

In free states, restaurants and independent, privately run stores (that is, non–state owned) must buy product from what we call a distributor. Distributors (some call them the middlemen) buy product from the supplier. Distributors in both the control states and the free states will encourage bars and restaurants to carry the brands they represent. The difference in the control state is that a bar or restaurant can't actually place an order for the product with a distributor—instead, they have to go to the state-run store. Here's an easier graphic to understand how your whiskey gets to your favorite venue:

CONTROL STATE, FOUR-TIERED SYSTEM
Producer/Distiller
➔➔ State Agency
➔➔ Distributor (who encourages and pushes product, but can't really sell)
➔➔ Store/Restaurant/Bar

FREE STATE, THREE-TIERED SYSTEM
Producer/Distiller
➔➔ Distributor (sells to)
➔➔ Store/Restaurant/Bar

I want you to understand the complexity behind how whiskey gets on the shelf so that you know why you may or may not see certain brands. A Philadelphia restaurateur once asked me to help her get a bottle of Glenfiddich 21 Rum Finish Single Malt Scotch. A distributor representative helped us locate the only remaining bottle statewide in Pittsburgh, hundreds of miles away. The state (control) bought only a few bottles and spread them miles away in different state-run stores. We put a special order in to have it sent from Pittsburgh to Philadelphia. Meanwhile, over the Ben Franklin Bridge and ten minutes into free-state New Jersey, the product was available. State-run liquor authorities make it illegal for stores and restaurants to buy out-of-state, though.

The bottom line is that when you can't find a bottle, there's a complicated network of systems in play. It could be that your state chose not to carry it, the brand doesn't have enough bottles to sell in all fifty states (so they choose a few key places to penetrate), the store doesn't like it, the bartender or beverage director hates it, or that it's so popular it flies off the self. These are the elements I contend with when I make recommendations to my students, and as I've compiled the lists in this book. It's a balancing act of availability, value, and deliciousness.

## TABLE 4: BANG FOR YOUR BUCK STARTER COLLECTION

| STYLE | COST | BRAND SUGGESTIONS | COMMENTS |
|---|---|---|---|
| Single Malt Scotch, Nonpeated | $45–$60 | Choose Two<br>Glenfiddich 12, 15<br>GlenDronach 12, 15<br>The Balvenie 12 DoubleWood<br>Auchentoshan 12<br>Glenmorangie 10<br>Old Pulteney 12<br>The Macallan 10 Fine Oak | There are many iconic "big brands" listed. I don't subscribe to the idea that small is better. These are respected, historic, award-winning whiskeys. I own all of them. You can find these just about anywhere. |

| STYLE | COST | BRAND SUGGESTIONS | COMMENTS |
|---|---|---|---|
| Single Malt, Peated | $50–$60 | Choose One<br>Bowmore 12<br>Ardbeg 10<br>Laphroaig 10<br>Highland Park 12<br>Springbank<br>Talisker 10 | Unless you discover you are an absolute peat fanatic, pick only one—it's a spice, not a mainstay. |
| Bourbon | $15–$40 | Choose Two<br>W. L. Weller (any release)<br>Four Roses Yellow Label<br>Four Roses Small Batch<br>Very Old Barton 90 or 100 proof<br>Buffalo Trace<br>Basil Hayden's<br>Eagle Rare Single Barrel 10<br>Rebel Yell Small Batch<br>Wild Turkey 101 Proof<br>Wild Turkey Russell's Reserve<br>Evan Williams Single Barrel<br>Colonel E. H. Taylor Small Batch<br>Ancient Age<br>Elijah Craig 12<br>Elmer T. Lee<br>Old Grand-Dad<br>Old Forester<br>Woodford Reserve<br>Bulleit<br>Angel's Envy<br>Michter's US 1<br>Knob Creek Single Barrel 9 YO | Ignore the hype surrounding some brands and check out these amazing buys. Many are made by the Kentucky "Big Boys," like Buffalo Trace, Four Roses, and Heaven Hill. All demonstrate a great bourbon profile: balanced, floral, and bursting with vanillas, coconuts, and toffees. |

| STYLE | COST | BRAND SUGGESTIONS | COMMENTS |
|---|---|---|---|
| Rye | $15–$40 | Choose One<br>Old Overholt<br>Rittenhouse Rye 100 proof<br>Wild Turkey Rye 80 proof<br>Michter's Rye<br>Russell's Reserve 6 Year Rye<br>Knob Creek Rye | These ryes make particularly great cocktails; I recommend them on ice if not in cocktails. |
| Irish Whiskey, Single Malt | $35–$50 | Choose One<br>Tullamore Dew 10<br>Knappogue Castle 12 Single Malt<br>The Tyrconnell Single Malt<br>Bushmills Blend<br>Tullamore Dew Blend | Premium Irish whiskeys like pot still and single malts get expensive fast. No need to do that yet. These are all great approachable, drinkable Irish whiskeys to start with. |
| Japanese Whisky | $70–$80 | Choose One<br>Yamazaki 12 or Hakushu 12<br>Nikka Taketsuru 12 Pure Malt | Choose Hakushu for a slightly peated offering; Yamazaki for more floral, cask, and spice; Nikka for slightly peated, coffee, and chocolate notes. |
| Small Artisanal Distiller, American Whiskey | $50–$60 | Choose Two Whiskeys from These Distillers (They'll Have a Range)<br>Kings County Spirits<br>Tuthilltown Spirits<br>Corsair Distillery<br>Catskills Distilling<br>Balcones Distilling<br>High West Distillery<br>Hillrock Estate Distillery<br>St. George Spirits<br>Kentucky Bourbon Distillers (Willett, Noah's Mill, Rowan's Creek)<br>Anchor Distilling Company (Old Potrero)<br>Westland Distillery<br>Long Island Spirits<br>Koval Distillery<br>Widow Jane Distilling (Bloody Butcher variants especially) | These are all grain-to-bottle distillers, doing everything on site. |

For this starter collection, I've created a realistic list that includes many brands you should be able to find and afford. Sure, I'd love to encourage you to find a non–chill filtered independent bottling of a sixteen-year-old Mortlach for your starter collection, but how realistic would that be? It might send you calling twenty-five purveyors you found online. The list below is exactly where I'd start if I were beginning again. I'll update the list on my Web site regularly (www.Heather greene.com).

I also write these words knowing thousands of e-mails will be sent to me or my publisher by angry whiskey trolls wondering how I "forgot" a brand they like—but hey, you need to start *somewhere*. Most important, these are all styles you can pair with food, use in cocktails, and drink neat or on the rocks.

Here are a few whiskies you can pepper into your collection when you're feeling flush. I have these myself, too.

### Single Malt Scotch
Scapa 16
GlenDronach 15
The Balvenie 14 Caribbean Rum Cask
The Balvenie 21 PortWood
Glenmorangie Nectar D'or or 18
Glenmorangie Ealanta or Signet
Abelour A'bunadh
Old Pulteney 17
Auchentoshan Valinch
Cragganmore's Distillers Edition
Laphroaig 18
Oban Distillers Edition or 14
Highland Park 18
Lagavulin Distillers Edition

**AMERICAN WHISKEY**
Blanton's
Colonel E. H. Taylor
High West Rendezvous Rye
Jim Beam's Signature Craft 12 YO
Masterson's Rye 10
Michter's 10 Bourbon or Rye

**JAPANESE**
Yamazaki 18
Nikka 17
Hibiki

**IRISH**
Redbreast 15
Knappogue Castle 16
Bushmills 16
Green Spot
Connemara

**REST OF WORLD DISTILLERS**
Brenne (France)
Mackmyra (Sweden)
Amrut (India)
Kavalan (Taiwan)

## JUST HOW EXPENSIVE IS WHISKEY?

Compared with beer, vodka, or wine, whiskey requires a long
inventory (maturation) time—money is essentially wrapped up

in those barrels sitting in warehouses. In addition, supply for matured spirit is not elastic; that is, a distiller can't respond instantaneously to extra demand. Increased demand with a somewhat fixed supply will always lead to higher prices. And some of that whiskey is lost during evaporation, too. Distillers look at angel's share as money vaporizing right out the window.

Taking into consideration all that maturation time (i.e., extra production costs) I think whiskey can be a downright good value. If we compare a $50 bottle of whiskey with a $15 bottle of wine, the cost is actually the same per ounce. But with wine, you'll polish off that bottle within a day or two. Your whiskey bottle will last longer. With vodka you'll probably be adding mixers, which should be taken into consideration when you think about the overall cost.

## PRICE PER OUNCE AND ML OF ALCOHOL BY LIQUID (USING 1 OUNCE = 29.5735 ML)

|  | WHISKEY | WINE | VODKA | BEER* |
|---|---|---|---|---|
| Cost in dollars | $50 | $15 | $30 | $10 |
| ABV | 40% | 12% | 40% | 5% |
| ml of alcohol | 300 | 90 | 300 | 106.45 |
| Cost per ml | $0.17 | $0.17 | $0.10 | $0.09 |
| Cost per ounce | $4.93 | $4.93 | $2.96 | $2.78 |
| *Beer = 6-pack of 12-ounce bottles | | | | |

## I'M NOT TELLING YOU HOW OLD I AM

Distillers in a hurry to meet the demand for whiskey have opted to drop age statements and now bottle whiskey that is younger than what they bottled just a few years ago—and it's happening a lot. Basil Hayden's eight-year-old whiskey, for example, is now just Basil Hayden. Some brands never used an age statement in the first place (I've recommended many of those brands in this book). In Scotland, the non–age statement bottle has been around for a long time in the form of blended Scotch— Johnnie Walker Blue carries no age statement. The luxury brand The Macallan broke tradition in 2013 by releasing a rare non–age statement expression called M that costs almost $4,000.

I am of two minds when it comes to brands' releasing non–age statement (NAS) whiskeys. On the one hand, too many consumers focus on age only and mistakenly believe that more time in the cask means a better whiskey. You know now that this is not true. Whiskeys made in America generally reach maturity when they are younger than Scotches, for example. And you also know now what type of whiskeys you like, and whether their flavor profile comes from spending more or less time sitting in a cask. So NAS whiskeys, then, require us to think about palate rather than focus on the age of the whiskey and our expectations of what that whiskey should or shouldn't taste like. I tasted the M and it was fantastic. I still have no idea how old the vatted whiskeys were in that bottle and I don't really care. What I do remember is that the rich, luxurious, silky, and mouthwatering notes like spice, chocolate, and orange made me very happy.

The freedom to use young and old whiskeys without having to think about an age statement on the front of the label allows distillers to harmonize flavors to their heart's content, and I'm all for that. Sometimes the addition of a young cask into a vat is exactly what the "recipe" needs. As I look at whiskeys on my own shelf, a good half of them don't list an age statement—I chose them based both on flavor and on the distillery's reputation for quality product.

On the downside, a distillery's temptation to release whiskey that would otherwise taste much better sitting in wood for more time can lead them to release something that may not be ready. My advice? If you notice a whiskey drop an age statement, go ahead and try it—see if the change in flavor is something you are okay with.

A related tip: Make sure that when you see a number listed on the bottle, it is followed by the word "year." I know I'm getting really detailed here, but some distillers have eliminated the word "year" on a few of their bottles and have left only the number on the label. It's a clever little trick to catch your eye!

## DISTILLERS EDITIONS, LIMITED EDITIONS, SPECIAL BOTTLINGS, SPECIAL RELEASES . . .

I can't think of a distiller—large or small—that doesn't create some sort of special release. And here's the truth: Even I get boggled sometimes by everything out there. Special editions, limited editions, and special bottlings all require a little digging around to figure out what's in the bottle that's different from the normal offering a distillery releases. Sometimes it's a temporary package change only.

Read the bottle labels to sleuth whether it's a commemorative, decorative bottle with the "same old" inside, or a newly designed bottle with a whole new whiskey inside as well. Both are respectable purchases: You might love a bottle's new look so much that you don't care what's inside: For example, I wish I had the Michter's decanter, with the shape of King Tut's head, that was released in the late 1970s. If you are ever in Kentucky, there is one on display at the Oscar Getz Museum of Whiskey History in Frankfort, along with hundreds of other silly bottle designs. Woodford Reserve sells its core-range whiskey in specially designed horse-themed bottles during the Kentucky Derby. But it also might mean that the whiskey inside changes from the usual whiskey a distillery releases, rather than merely releasing a new bottle design with its contents unchanged. Maybe it's a different maturation process, or a change during vatting. It could be anything that changes nuance flavor while still maintaining its "house style." I always look out for these kinds of special bottles from my favorite brands—they are a great opportunity to taste a variation of a whiskey I like a lot already.

**Just Because It's on the Label Doesn't Mean It's a Real Style**

You'll see all sorts of special editions released with words like "double malt" or "straight malt" or words that *sound* like regulated styles of whiskey. Other overused words you'll see written are "craft" and "handmade." Be aware of how marketing can mislead you about an actual style of whiskey. I saw double malt bourbon on a shelf last week. Bourbon? That's a type of whiskey I know. Double malt? I don't know what that is—it's something the distiller made up to catch my eye. Think twice when you read something on a label you've never seen or heard of before. "Craft" is a vague word that can be used to suggest a way a whiskey is made when it's not.

## "CORE RANGE" EXPLAINED

"Core range" usually refers to the most popular, classic group of whiskeys sold by a company. Most of what you see at stores or in bars are the distillery's core range of whiskeys: Glenlivet 12, Balvenie DoubleWood 12, Four Roses Yellow Label, for example. Many brands, such as The Macallan, release their core-range whiskeys (10, 12, 18); a line of something different, like their newish Fine Oak range (15, 17, 21); a Fine and Rare portfolio; and other arty limited-edition whiskeys, like their Masters of Photography Series, a chic bottling featuring Annie Leibovitz photos. Core-range whiskeys will probably look familiar to you. The special editions, limited editions, or new ranges, as in The Macallan's Fine Oak series, will stand out because the packaging will change a bit.

## Do These Special Bottles Taste Good?

Many limited editions are little puff-of-smoke gems that disappear off shelves almost as quickly as they hit. Some of them are downright amazing. *Whisky Advocate* named the 2012 Four Roses Limited Edition Small Batch release American Whiskey of the Year, and the 2013 125th anniversary edition from the same distillery was an instant sellout. You can find a bottle now only on the black market, on sites like Craigslist. My first taste of a Distillers Edition, the Lagavulin 16 Distillers Edition it's called, catapulted my appreciation of Islay whiskies tenfold. The sherry butt maturation pushing through the peat smoke offered more complexity than any other Islay I had tried, including the core-range variant, Lagavulin 16. The Glenfiddich Snow Phoenix Distillers Edition, a sweeter, creamier Glenfiddich expression produced out of salvaged casks nearly lost after a freak snowstorm fell on warehouses in Dufftown, Scotland, is delicious. It came in a sexy black box and sold out within eight months or so, never to be reproduced.

### WHISKEY FOR SPORTS LOVERS

Like basketball and whiskey both? I do! That's why I wish I had a bottle of that limited edition Maker's Mark with coach John Calipari's head printed on the outside of it, released in 2010. Yeah, sure it's a little goofy, but Calipari coached UMass basketball when I attended, so that particular limited edition bottle represents a little alumni pride, even though the liquid inside is the same as the regular bottle I have sitting on my shelf already. And that's exactly the point of the limited edition bottle: to emotionally get you excited about the brand.

## Limited Edition Costs

I think limited edition whiskeys should cost no more than $200—and there are good ones that cost less than $100. Beyond the $200 price point, however, I feel that's moving into a more vintage or "rare" category than a limited edition. Whiskey's very expensive limited editions should have the whole package: It should be a new variant with flavor complexity, luxurious texture, a lingering finish, and age. Some of those virtues (not all) I might overlook in a less-expensive limited edition whiskey. Many Scotch limited edition expressions are now being released NAS, in which case you must rely on the variants you've tried before from the distiller. Soon, you'll start to have your own favorite distillers that you won't mind taking more of a gamble on when they release special bottles.

### HOW TO BUY A DISTILLERS EDITION IN FIVE EASY STEPS

1. Make sure you've discovered a couple of whiskey distillers or brands you like.
2. Decide on your budget.
3. Go to your favorite liquor store or look online to see what special editions your favorite distiller is offering, and then do a little research.
4. If the whiskey is a new style or variant from your favorite distillery and you can afford it, give it a go! If the limited edition is a package change only and the outside label painting or etching is of your favorite coach, model, car, or Egyptian mummy, that's cool, too. People collect all sorts of things in life, right?

5. Go home and open the bottle; take a taste. Enjoy it or curse me. If the bottle looks wacky, put it on your mantelpiece under your moose head. If you've just found a new style you love, impress guests by serving them something they have never heard of.

## CHEAP WAYS TO TASTE THE GOOD STUFF

Whiskey can be downright expensive, but let's look at a few ways to sample pricey whiskeys without investing in an entire bottle right away.

### Brands Want to Talk to You (Might as Well Take Advantage of That)

By now, you probably have an idea of what whiskeys you generally like and have found a few brands you are gravitating toward. But do you know how much the distillers of these same brands want to speak with you? Millions of dollars are at stake here—brand strategists celebrate success by driving the right consumer to their product. Use this to your advantage. Thousands of free whiskey tastings, loyalty programs, and special events happen in your town or places you might visit on vacation—all are free or at a low cost to you. At The Flatiron Room, big-distillery representatives drop by to enjoy the atmosphere as much as they do to host free events for whiskey loyalists. Don't perceive these marketing tactics too cynically. You have something to gain—more knowledge and free samples! Yet very few people take advantage of these great opportunities. I've been to many sparsely attended events, presented by master distillers who have flown in rare and precious whiskeys of extremely coveted brands from Kentucky or Scotland. Sign up for loyalty programs, too, and keep in touch with your favorite spirits maker to find out when there may be a tasting near you. Keep in mind that brand-funded events showcase only their own babies, so you'll have to crash a bunch if you'd like to taste a variety.

## Whiskey Joints

Whiskey rooms such as The Flatiron Room offer very expensive whiskeys in tasting flights. This saves you money and protects you from awful mistakes—you won't find yourself investing in a plonk bottle. Sampling flights are par for the course at whiskey-specific establishments, and any good whiskey venue, lounge, bar, or restaurant will probably let you have a reasonable taste of something. *Reasonable.* Please don't get carried away by that suggestion. I don't mean for you to go in and ask for a bunch of freebies or a Glenlivet 25. But by all means, use the knowledge you've gotten in this book to indulge your curiosity about a few brands and then eventually settle down with one or two for the night. Just remember, leave a nice tip for the waiter.

### HOW TO ORDER AT THE BAR

Don't be shy. Belly up to the bar and order your favorite dram exactly the way you want it. Here's how.

"*On the rocks.*" You will be served a pour of your whiskey on ice. Do you feel uncomfortable ordering ice in your whiskey, even though you secretly enjoy it that way? Don't fret. We'll talk about ice in a bit. Shaming anyone for a whiskey on the rocks order is taboo in my book. Literally.

"*Neat.*" Your bartender will pour you a dram of whiskey without any ice.

*"Neat with a side of water."* Some finer establishments will offer little water droppers or wee little water pitchers, which are commonplace in Scotland. A small amount of water is said to "open the flavors" of your Scotch. Some like to add it, some don't. Your choice. Use a straw or spoon if you are handed a pint of water; it makes it easier to add just the right amount.

*"One ice cube, please."* Some whiskey drinkers love just the slight chill of one ice cube, and the perfect teeny amount of water as the ice cube melts into the whiskey over time.

*"Rittenhouse Rye old-fashioned, please."* Go ahead and call out your favorite whiskey when you order a cocktail, if you'd like.

*"Could you recommend something?"* Good bartenders want you to feel comfortable at their bar and most love talking about cocktails and spirits. Ask them what they've recently enjoyed and see if you don't discover something new. Or, let them know a particular style you like and let them pick out something for you.

## IDENTIFYING WHISKEY VALUE, OR, DO YOU HAVE EXPENSIVE (BLIND) TASTE?

The tastings you have done to this point have been influenced by the fact that you know what you're drinking. Blind tastings are a whole new challenge and a great way to fine-tune your palate. And there is no better way to start being able to identify great value in a whiskey. The price, a brand's fairy-tale story, or someone else's notes won't be able to persuade you.

Blind tastings—which I will teach you how to do—encourage you to use your brain in new ways. The power of expectation and its influence on our perception of taste and aroma disappear in a blind tasting, letting us establish a more honest relationship with what's in our glass. It is one of the most pure and enjoyable ways to discover your true palate, explore what your preferences are, and describe what you like more confidently in a store or restaurant.

When novices and self-professed whiskey experts attend my blind tastings, I notice something interesting: After I serve them a flight of whiskey without telling them exactly what they are drinking, the novices get busy identifying aromas, excited about their newfound passion, while the "experts" sit and try endlessly to guess the exact whiskey they are drinking and which ones are the rarest or most expensive. They struggle: "I should know this!" they shout. I've actually seen dozens of grown men fist pump the air when I announce that their favorite selection in a blind tasting was the oldest Scotch. I ask them what makes them think they just won something, and then pour extra whiskey for everyone else but them because they missed the point.

I once conducted two blind tastings that included the much-talked-about and heralded Pappy Van Winkle I wrote about in chapter 3. My own challenge in conducting this blind tasting was to select whiskeys that I thought would stack well in a blind lineup next to Pappy, which is a delicious bourbon for sure. I chose a range of some well-reviewed bourbons with various profiles like Michter's 10, Blanton's Single Barrel, Jefferson's Reserve Very Small Batch, and Basil Hayden's—all whiskeys that I truly enjoy. The tasters that night included journalists, chefs, bakers, whiskey aficionados, and whiskey novices alike.

Fairly quickly into both events, preferences started to emerge, and the whiskey beginners led the way. By the end of the first tasting, a whopping 80 percent of the group selected the Jefferson's and the Michter's for having the best overall nose and taste, whereas a second group put Jefferson's, Michter's, and Blanton's Single Barrel at a near tie. Everyone was shocked: "Pappy didn't 'win'?" Not during my blind tasting sessions.

Social dynamics can influence a group blind tasting—so pay attention to how your own attitude might change when someone speaks to you about his or her preferences. An outspoken professional chef in one of my blind tastings commented that he didn't like a particular dram, and it seemed as though he tilted others in his direction. An influential writer declared her favorite pour and no doubt pulled others in her direction. I was able to eliminate price, label, and prestige of the whiskey from the equation, but I hadn't taken into account the dynamics of the group.

I blind taste all the time. I'm not kidding: with soda pop, gin and tonics, chocolate, and beer—you name it. It's a game that my husband plays, too. You can do it *anywhere*, on your kitchen stools, at the bar, in a restaurant. Taste two things without knowing what they are and make a judgment: *I like that one.* One night my cheap-ass husband bought what I declared was a "shitty" gin for our gin and tonics. I mistakenly made that assumption (shame on me!) based solely on price and packaging. He challenged me to a blind tasting "gin off" between his twenty-buck purchase and my highbrow hooch stashed in the freezer. As it turns out, his—a juniper-y, pungent, piney, cheap London dry gin—cut through the tonic better and gave us that "by-the-beach" taste we both were yearning for during a New York City heat wave. If he whispered, "I told you so," he was smart enough to do it in our dog's ear.

Do blind tastings with whiskey as often as you can. Order a couple of whiskeys at the local bar with some friends and split the bill equally. Taste a few cheaper ones and more expensive ones. Get creative; choose all bourbons or all ryes or a mix of a bunch of styles and prices. Put different whiskeys in your Manhattan or old-fashioned. Sharpening your palate is how you will really be able to identify value. *The most important thing to remember is that the price of a whiskey is not always proportionately related to the taste of the whiskey.*

### How to Hold a Blind Palate-Discovery Tasting

For these blind tastings you will need a partner (or group of friends) to pour and keep track of the whiskey lineup. I've uploaded a series of tasting mats on my Web site, so feel free to print out one for the event if it will make it easier for you. For this tasting, you'll want to narrow down which whiskey style you'd like to explore more in depth—bourbon or single malts.

Your first blind tasting will be about identifying value. I define value as "bang for your buck"—just because a whiskey is triple the amount of money or is hard to find doesn't mean that it's triple the flavor. You'll discover whether your palate really thinks it's worth the money to spend a few dollars more for a certain whiskey—sometimes it is. Many of my students are happy to discover that their favorite whiskey is the one sold for less money.

For this tasting, you will pour a series of whiskeys at different price ranges but with similar taste profiles. I don't recommend you taste a peated malt within a blind-bourbon series, for example. All the whiskeys in this tasting are ones I like very much, despite their price or age. Also, the whiskeys in a series should have the same ABV range, plus or minus 5 percent. I learned early on how a whiskey with a high ABV skews an evaluator's opinion—sometimes a taster will wince and cry "Way too strong!" You can do this tasting in groups of three or six, depending on how extensive you want to get.

Designate someone to pour the whiskeys in a row horizontally (if you're doing three) or in rows of three on top of one another (so that you can fit them all on the tasting mat I mentioned earlier). Make sure to keep track of which whiskey is which. Choose identical glasses. It is also important to use some kind of markers if you don't use a tasting mat. Blue painter's tape attached to the bottom of the glass can work well, too. Just write the name down on the tape, or a number that corresponds to the name of the whiskey you poured and kept on a separate list. Once you start picking up a couple of whiskeys, you may very well lose track of the order and then have to start over.

## Five-Step Blind Tasting

1. Once the whiskeys are organized in front of you in rows, nose all of them. Take the time to get the initial aromas off of the drams, and then go back and forth among the different whiskeys.

2. Hold one whiskey in your right hand and one whiskey in your left, and move them back and forth, both of them, alternating placing them under your nose. Try to identify some of the aromatic properties we discussed: Do you nose almonds? Vanilla? Cloves?

3. Evaluate if any of the whiskeys begin to stand out to you right away. Start to get an architecture of what your immediate preferences might be, and don't overthink it too much. Try to nose the whiskey with your mouth open, to get as many aromatics as possible.

4. Taste all of the whiskeys, starting from glass number 1, and see if any surprise you. Did one smell a certain way but actually taste completely different from what you expected? I love whiskeys that do that. Are any immediately off-putting to you? How is the finish, if there is any? Do any of the whiskeys give you cooling or heat sensation? Which is less giving of its aromatics?

5. Evaluate: Start eliminating glasses that aren't at the top of your list. Narrow down your choices to the top three. Peel back the results and see which whiskeys you like the most.

### BLIND BOURBON VALUE TASTING (APPROXIMATE COSTS)

Woodford Reserve Double Oaked Bourbon $60.00

Blanton's Single Barrel $50.00

Angel's Envy Bourbon $43.00

Michter's Bourbon US 1 $38.00

Evan Williams Single Barrel $28.00

Four Roses Yellow Label $20.00

BLIND SINGLE MALT WHISK(E)Y TASTING
The Macallan 18 $200.00
Glenfiddich 18 $90.00
Bushmills 16 Year Old Single Malt $79.99
Hakushu 12 $59.99
The Tyrconnell Irish Single Malt $34.99
Auchentoshan Classic $30.00

## Whiskey as Investment?

There was a lot of press coverage about investing in whiskey around the same time I held a whiskey dinner for a bunch of Lehman Brothers executives at The Palm in New York City. As I spoke about whiskey and led them through the tasting, a few of the guys started throwing whiskey on one another, splashing it recklessly against walls, tables, and a few angry dressed-up women. Two days later, news erupted that Lehman Brothers would fold, which I suppose gave the tasters ample time to both nurse the binge-drinking hangover and look for other asset-collecting opportunities.

That year (2008), there was a smattering of articles online and in outlets like CNNMoney about whiskey as an investment. "Liquid gold," they called it. Now the topic is a full-blown conversation, sparked by a 2011 headline-grabbing press release from the whiskey evaluation experts at Whisky Highland (www.whiskyhighland.com) that claimed if you'd invested in the top ten performing whiskey brands in 2008, you would have achieved a gain of more than 400 percent. This cracked open a heated debate between whiskey moralists who eschew whiskey stock hoarding and thoughtful collectors who claim it shouldn't matter to you whether they drink the whiskey or put it on a shelf for years. Either way, you don't get the bottle, they say. But the truth is, how whiskey is collected by a few can really have an impact on the rest of us.

With the current scarcity of some American whiskey brands, opportunists scour liquor stores for miles searching for any new release they think might increase in cost and buy as much as they can. Essentially, they function as scalpers. The result is a healthy black market for whiskey and more impetus for distillers to raise prices because consumers haven't shown much price sensitivity as bottle costs slowly creep up. Also partly to blame for the black market in whiskey is the tiered structure of how liquor is bought and sold in the United States. All product must flow through a distributor from the importer or whiskey maker before hitting a bar or liquor store, so it's technically illegal for anyone to sell liquor privately.

Much of the black market buying and selling in America right now is what I'd call small potatoes: little whiskey flips that get a scalper a couple hundred bucks or so a pop. When the Four Roses 125th Anniversary Limited Edition hit the market with a retail price of $85, scalpers quickly swooped in on the release, and within months the sold-out bottles appeared on Craigslist for $350. You might argue that it's pretty good money, but can you imagine what kind of time commitment that kind of business requires of scalpers? I once received the lowdown from this sort of "collector," who basically told me it amounted to spending weeks in a car and hitting every small liquor store from New York to Ohio. Black market collectors are on the phone constantly and even give small gifts to shop owners so that they remember to call them when a "special stash" arrives. "Make some cookies," someone once told me. No, thanks.

Whiskey sold at auctions in reputable auction houses like Bonhams, Sotheby's, and Christie's is an entirely different story, though: Here is where you're more likely to rub shoulders with skilled and passionate whiskey collectors bidding on bottles of rare Scotch that can reach upward of hundreds of thousands of dollars. What separates these whiskey whales from the small-potato whiskey flippers is their deep knowledge of the industry, brands, history, past performance of particular bottles, and their willingness to sit on a bottle of whiskey for a decade. And, of course, they have enough money to invest with comfort. I was very heavily involved with auctions when I worked at Glenfiddich, whose total value of single collectible bottles sold at auction in the U.K. reached more than $800,000 in 2013. My role was to connect potential buyers with the bottles up for bidding, to host tastings, and to work with the press to communicate the rarity and provenance of the bottles. Today I'll work independently, offering to consult, very carefully, quietly, and in partnership with individual buyers. Most bidders in this arena wish to remain anonymous, often sending an assistant to make their bids while they remain connected via cell phone in real time. If you are curious about the best-performing whiskeys in the world, check out www.whiskyhighland.co.uk. The site regularly updates what they call the Whisky Highland Index, a ranking of distillers producing top collectible bottles. The data takes into account the following four variables: auction bottle price, highest single bottle price, average price per collectible bottle, and highest percent gain in value over time.

### "But *I'm* the Most Expensive!"

Single malt Scotch whisky The Dalmore was the first whisky to break six figures on the auction floor with the release of a whisky called Trinitas in 2010. The bottle contained a vatting of whiskies aged up to 140 years old. Since then, Scotch brands look to one-up one another in the press with stories of bottles reaching astronomical prices. The current Guinness world record for the highest price fetched at auction goes to The Macallan with the 2010 sale of a $460,000 rare whisky bottled in a French Lalique crystal decanter. The 2012 world record accolade came two years after the sale in response to Glenfiddich, which claimed in 2012 that it was *its* $94,000 bottle of the Janet Sheed Roberts that was the most expensive whisky ever sold. The team—of which I was a part at the time—claimed that the cost of the fancy Lalique decanter shouldn't count. The whiskey drama unfolded in the press, and reputable outlets like National Public Radio covered the story with send-up segments titled things like "Update: This One Really Is the Most Expensive Whisky, We're Told!"

While collecting is serious business, some of the attention-seeking tactics surrounding it provide fodder for a laugh. Here's more: In late 2012, a single malt Scotch whisky distillery called Tomintoul released a giant 4-foot 9-inch bottle of whiskey weighing 105 liters and the capacity to serve more than 50,000 drams. While it was expected to reach between £100,000 and £150,000, the whisky failed to reach its minimum reserve—you can now find the behemoth standing naively and proudly in Edinburgh at the Scotch Whisky Experience, a Disney-like tourist attraction where little carnival carts on tracks take you through wax figurines, bagpipe music, and now, I suppose, a giant bottle of whisky. Don't miss it. The Famous Grouse later created a bottle that surpasses even that in showmanship—it stands 5½ feet tall and can serve more than 9,000 drams of whisky. Coney Island–style spectacles can wow even the most "civilized" of Scotch fans. Come to think of it, I once paid $2 to see "the tiniest woman in the world"—so there you go.

My rule for investing in whiskey is quite simple. Find what you love and buy two—one to drink and one to save in the event the whiskey changes, increases in price, or ceases to exist. Don't flip whiskey. Short-term speculation is a gamble and a whiskey-collecting practice without soul. Thoughtful, long-term investment in bottles that you love or hope to pass on to your children is a totally different ball game, though, should you find yourself with thousands (!) of dollars you want to play with. But *really* know your stuff. Knowing what you like is a good start.

I won't tell you what to invest in here, but instead I will share with you some tips on *how* you might approach the idea of investment should you be interested:

1. Buy what you drink—should the market bottom out, you'll be left with something you can enjoy at the very least.

2. Collect whiskeys from high-performing distilleries. You can find these on www.whiskyhighland.co.uk and www.worldwhiskyindex.com.

3. Stick with limited-run bottles (limited editions, special editions), which should offer higher returns, rather than the core range a distillery has on offer. That said, even the core-range prices have increased over the past couple of years.

## STORAGE

Luckily for us whiskey lovers, we don't need to be as careful with our spirit as we are with our wines. Once whiskey is opened, we've got a bit of time to polish off the bottle before we can notice any differences in taste (I'll get into the "how long" shortly). Even after a long time has passed, you have to be fairly skilled with nosing and tasting to really identify the changes that are happening on a molecular level and affecting aromatic compounds that reach your palate. Below are my own guidelines I follow, starting with how I store unopened bottles of whiskey and then how I handle the open bottles (hint: Drink them).

### AGING: WHISKEY VERSUS WINE

"So what you are telling me is that whiskey, then, is like a woman who has just arrived in New York—she's fresh, eager, and ready to please—but after twelve years aging here she can become fucked up."

Once again, the poetic genius of a New York hedge-fund manager can be so touching and relevant. But he's right—at least, when it comes to Scotch whisky. And it's the years spent aging in the cask (or, in Wall Street layman's terms, getting "fucked up") that give whiskey most of its flavor. Wine ages in a bottle, whiskey does not—the moment you take a whiskey out of a cask, it stops aging. Remember, the age statement on a bottle of whiskey is a promise to you that its contents are no younger than the stated age, although you may find whiskeys that are actually older than the age statement. That's within the rules. A whiskey maker often looks for consistency, so if that means pulling an older cask for completing the taste profile, then so be it. A Kentucky distiller once said to me, "If you start making a shitty bourbon, you better just keep on making a shitty bourbon for the rest of your life 'cause there's nothing more important than consistency."

Let me repeat that an old whiskey does not mean that it's a better whiskey. In general, younger whiskeys reveal the aromatics that develop in distillation fermentation. The wood aromatics pop the longer a whiskey stays in a cask. So in some ways it's a question of taste. The aging question depends on style, too. Whiskey aged in first fill or virgin oak will be ready for bottling at an earlier age than a single malt Scotch or other whiskey using refill casks.

## Avoid Temperature Extremes

To be safe, I keep my bottles stored at room temperature, between 60 and 69 degrees. I don't have a basement, but if I did, I might keep my whiskey there. Anywhere you can keep whiskey from extreme temperature fluctuations is a good place to store the bottle. While the extent to which temperature affects properly sealed liquid is debated by whiskey aficionados and whiskey makers, I don't recommend leaving your whiskey in the trunk of a car during a heat wave and forgetting about it, something I did a couple of years back. Even though I couldn't tell a difference when I served it up on ice, I still wouldn't recommend this knuckleheaded whiskey storage method. In terms of very cold temperatures—freezing even—cold is preferable to extreme heat, but try to avoid it. My cold is better than hot theory is based on two things: First, I like to drink Hakushu 12 Japanese malt out of the freezer, a tip introduced to me while I was in Japan, and second, when New Zealand scientists uncovered two crates of one-hundred-year-old whiskey buried in Arctic permafrost in 2007, the thawed contents was deemed "a gift from heaven," according to Richard Paterson, whiskey blender for The Dalmore. Since then, a company called Shackleton, named after the British explorer who abandoned his ship—and whiskey—has carefully recreated the taste of the spirit in bottles you can go out and buy today.

## Avoid Light

UV rays will get into your spirit and change the contents of your bottle, too. So while you're at it with keeping it away from temperature changes, keep it out of light as well.

## Store Upright

Keep your bottles standing upright—the exact opposite way you store wine. One reason for this practice is that the high level of alcohol in your whiskey could erode the cork. I've seen my fair share of crumbly cork bits floating around in old whiskey bottles (not mine). The second reason for this is to prevent any leakage. Once opened, your bottle is at risk of leaking through the top where the cork or cap meets the glass neck.

## Avoid Oxidation

Wine oxidizes at a tremendous rate, which is why you must drink it soon after opening the bottle. Whiskey oxidizes very slowly over time, but it will still oxidize to some extent nonetheless. Whiskey and wine oxidation occurs when the liquid is exposed to oxygen. Oxygen ($O_2$) essentially "steals" electrons from a compound within the liquid, thereby changing the substance. I should mention here that oxygen isn't a requirement for oxidation in the purely chemical definition—any loss of electrons when two substances meet is considered an oxidative reaction. But oxygen is a great oxidative agent. Confused? Don't be. All I'm really trying to tell you is that you have a certain amount of time before oxygen gets into your whiskey, wreaking havoc on a molecular level and changing the overall flavor.

The more oxygen that is present in your bottle, the more opportunity for oxidation. If your opened bottle is two-thirds full or so, I'd drink it within a year. When my whiskeys dip below the halfway mark, I move them onto the "drink me now" shelf, and anyone who comes to my place is welcome to the stash.

Something else to consider when you open and close your whiskey is that you'll lose some of the "top notes," or some of the lighter, fruitier floral notes that are the first aromatics. These top notes can hang in suspension, pretty aromatics floating around what's often the "whiskey headspace," or the area just above the liquid in your dram or bottle. The more you open and close your bottle, the more opportunity for aromatics in the headspace to fly away.

### Decanters

Use decanters when you plan to drink your whiskey within a year—decanters look beautiful on a shelf but can speed the rate at which the whiskey changes. Why? Because the seal is often less tight, allowing oxidation opportunities, and the light penetrates through them more easily. I actually keep my "everyday" whiskey in decanters. I also love the feel of pouring from them.

## Handling the Bottle

You don't have to be too precious about handling the bottle, admiring it, or showing it off to your friends. Whiskey can stand some manhandling. That said, I always get one smart aleck who asks, "Can I shake it?" The answer to that question is no. Don't shake your whiskey bottle like a cheap Champagne in the back of a stretch limo during a bachelorette party.

## GLASSWARE

With the advent of the whiskey and cocktail craze over the past decade—especially martinis—I notice that there is also an attitude that bigger is better. Not so fast. A pour of whiskey should peak at about 1½ ounces, and a martini-style, whiskey-based cocktail like a Manhattan should measure no more than 5 ounces. Anything more than that looks sloppy. Worse, your cocktail becomes warm in one of those ginormous martini glasses that I've seen at too many Mexican restaurants, filled to the brim with salt, tequila, and sour mix. It's too much. There really is a difference in taste over time.

If you feel like getting dainty or dorky—as I am sometimes wont to do—get yourself what is called a *Glencairn* whiskey glass. These are fabulous for evaluating and appreciating a fine whiskey. They can even come with a little glass lid that protects the aromatics from escaping too quickly and freely. The creators of the Glencairn (see illustration), a consortium of Scotch whisky aficionados based in Scotland, developed the shape and size to best enhance the flavors of a whisky. The bulbous bottom collects all sorts of aromatics in its headspace, then filters them all up toward the thinner top portion of the glass, targeting your olfactory receptors "just so." You wouldn't want any of those molecules running wild out a wide-mouthed glass and escaping your evaluation, right?

For a feel-good factor, nothing beats a heavy Waterford or Christofle crystal–type tumbler for a whiskey. I love the weight of a glass like that

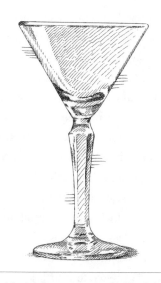

*Martini glasses can get too big. Don't feel like you have to fill the whole thing. A five-ounce drink is perfectly respectable.*

*A stemmed whiskey glass with a cap holds in aromas before tasting sessions begin. They are used by the überserious whiskey geeks, often on tasting panels.*

*Heavy crystal tumblers can be used for any kind of whiskey and are one of my favorite ways to drink whiskey.*

*The classic Glencairn glass, created by whiskey makers in Scotland, holds aromatics in the bulb of the glass. The narrow mouth focuses the aromatics for more targeted and effective nosing.*

in my hand, and men feel much more comfortable holding on to something with some gravitas. I get that. You don't necessarily need über-pricey Waterford, but check out the weights of lowballs, as they're often called. Choose one with some heft and personality to match the big bold bourbon or Scotch that will be poured into it.

I've never minded small wineglasses for whiskey, either. They are better than shot glasses, plastic tumblers, red keg cups, and pint glasses by a long shot. Wine sommeliers often say crystal is best, the unmistakable and appealing "clink" sound when you toast is so satisfying. Try not to choose colored wineglasses—or any colored glasses for that matter. A lot of whiskey appreciation comes down to the richness of color in your glass, and helps to prepare you for what's coming. Don't you want to see those rich oxblood reds of an aged thirty-year-old Scotch when it's offered to you? I do.

There really is no standardized way to serve whiskey—yet. And maybe that's okay. Whiskey is varied and so are our palates and styles. So when you are served whiskey in a restaurant, bar, or someone else's home, always look at the size of the glass and the amount of the pour. What's important is that you monitor the distance between your nose and the spirit before gently inhaling the aromas—remember, whiskey is 40 percent ABV *at least*, so do your nose a favor and look after it. If you are throwing your own party, don't overpour. If you've got a boozehound over, you can always offer seconds. Or thirds. Or switch him or her to beer.

## ICE VERSUS NO ICE—RECLAIMING THE DRINK FROM PURISTS

In 2009, *The Wall Street Journal* called me "less persnickety about ice" than Scotch purists like master blender Richard Paterson, who was known for flinging buckets of ice into his audience in a theatrical display of rancor for chilling a whiskey. This was my first big media mention, and it was not met with very kind words. Whiskey fundamentalists cried, "You are ruining the spirit!" and "You have no idea what you are talking about!" For the first five years I spent in the whiskey business, starting from the mid-2000s, some Scotch drinkers shook their heads disapprovingly and grunted like wild beasts when I even mentioned the word "ice." I was poked at, made fun of, batted around like a cat toy, discredited, and yelled at in front of large crowds for declaring my acceptance of ice in a whiskey.

As new whiskey fans entered the fold, spirit fundamentalism started to take a backseat. By 2010, classic whisky distillers like The Macallan celebrated the new whiskey drinker with an "ice plunge" event for bartenders who felt like diving into an ice-filled pool at the yearly cocktail conference "Tales of the Cocktail." State-of-the-art Macallan ice makers designed to mold perfectly clean, jewellike round spheres sit on back bars in many lounges. Today I get phone calls and e-mails from guys who want to talk to me about their "ice program." I know a couple of bars where a guest must wait for *twenty minutes* for the bartender to chip some ice off a large block. I order a pint in those places.

Ice will change the flavor of your whiskey, but is that necessarily a bad thing? When it is 95 degrees and humid in Manhattan, I want to hear the clink of ice falling into my glass, and I want to tone down the spice and "heat" of a whiskey. I'm looking to refresh and cool my palate rather than curl up with rich and warm aromatics like cinnamon and clove. Ice mellows a whiskey; it brings down the "pinging" of alcohol dancing on your tongue and elevates aromatics such as vanilla, white chocolate, and citrus. Essentially, the temperature determines which volatile molecules are bouncing out of your glass and into your nose. Enjoy whiskey for its dynamism, for its ability to take on an entirely different personality with ice.

### Here's When I Don't Use Ice

You know by now that I'm a big believer in the subjectivity involved in enjoying whiskey, and at the end of the day I'll support your drinking it however you want to drink it. Yet there is one case when you should think twice before plopping some cubes into your glass, and that is if someone pours you a rare or vintage whiskey. A thirty- or even forty-year-old Scotch displays an orchestra of flavors it has collected over all those years, and you will want to explore as many of those flavors as you are capable of detecting. The long, slow finish generates heat as it goes down the back of your palate, the trail of the leathery and dark-fruit flavors that follow—this is an experience that only a fine, aged whiskey can provide. It's a cocktail of flavors on its own, and ice will erase some of those treasures. I mention "Scotch" specifically here because most aged and rare whiskeys come from Scotland.

# 5

## Cocktails!

### *New and Classic Favorites*

NOW THAT YOU KNOW the basics of building your bar, it's time to start getting in there and shaking things up with some fabulous, whiskey-based cocktails.

### WHISKEY COCKTAIL BASICS

It's awesome to walk into a room with a pitcher of Manhattans for your guests predinner, or to serve a perfectly balanced old-fashioned to your partner at the end of a long day. For me, the ritual of cocktail making—meticulously peeling a fragrant fruit garnish, stirring with a bar spoon—both prepares my palate and acts as a bridge between a tough day and an easy evening. Creating a nice meal, wineglass in hand, relaxes some people, but mixing a drink is the main culinary event happening in my kitchen. The rest is takeout.

Many blogs, articles, and bartenders make the art of mixing drinks overly daunting and create the impression that mixing up a good drink requires years of skill and panache. There's a perfect "style" to shaking one, they'll say. (Go on YouTube and you'll catch a few videos that show the variety and theater surrounding a good shake. Up and down? Back and forth? With a smile or without? While walking? Double-handed shake? Dry shake?) I tended bar for years and shook without much thought beyond making sure I did it with vigor and the shaker was chilled.

Cocktail popularity has contributed to the rise in spirit consumption worldwide—and for that I'm thankful—but too many potentially great home bartenders are afraid to strike out on their own after seeing how elegantly a talented bartender can handle a bar spoon. I can see it in the eyes of my students in our cocktail-making class—they are downright terrified to look foolish. I spent twenty minutes during one cocktail-making class focusing solely on peeling a good solid lemon rind and another half hour teaching guests with fumbling fingers how to spin a bar spoon.

When you don't look like a pro, don't worry about it! Orr Shtuhl, who wrote *An Illustrated Guide to Cocktails*, suggests using a chopstick in a pinch. I'm all for it. Good technique looks great, but you don't need to obsess over it to make a great drink. I can't chop onions like Jean-Georges, but that doesn't keep me from making a killer salad and soup every once in a while. I'll give you tips on the special techniques that really matter for certain cocktails.

The most important elements in cocktail making are fresh ingredients and quality spirits in the right amounts, or finding good balance. A measuring device called a jigger will help you do that. A little too much citrus and your drink will be too acidic, overdo the simple syrup and the drink will taste sugary. Glassware choice is important, too. For martini-style drinks you'll want a glass no larger than five ounces. Low-ball drinks look and feel great in something with a little weight to them. I also look for unusual shapes and vintage finds. Honestly, you don't have to spend a fortune. I found a Don Draper–style set for ten bucks, complete with a silver rim and a chic metal storage device. People unload glassware all the time.

## Start with the Right Bar Tools

There are five essential tools you'll need to outfit the perfect home bar, and you can buy them all for less than $50. Of course, you could spend more if you wanted to, like you would if you wanted to buy high-end silverware, wineglasses, and dinnerware. But that's up to you.

*Boston Shaker*

*Boston shakers are often sold in complete sets at home goods stores. Use a tempered pint glass as a substitute if you want to shake it like a bartender does (pint glass not shown).*

This is a sixteen-ounce mixing glass that looks like a beer pint glass and fits into a larger, metal bar tin. It's the shaker your bartender probably uses. The mixing glass can be used alone to stir drinks like a Manhattan, or used in combination with the tin to shake your drinks. Sure, there are fancier shakers on the market, but I have better luck with the

Boston shaker. The seal can be so tight that you'll need to assertively tap the edge of the tin with the heel of your palm to release it. I like that tight seal: I'm clumsy, and find comfort in knowing the drink won't splatter all over the kitchen. No matter what kind of shaker you use, you'll need to use a strainer for pouring.

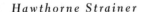

*Hawthorne Strainer*

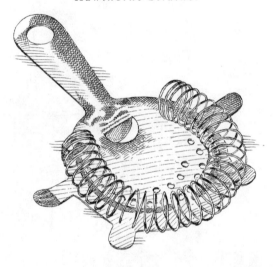

*Strainer*

This rounded tool with a handle and circular spring head will fit snugly over either the metal bar tin or the mixing glass so that as you pour, ice, fruit segments, or other large pieces won't fall into your cocktail. Use your pointer finger to hold it in place. Practice with water to get comfortable with it.

## *Jigger*

*Jigger*

The jigger measures your ingredients to help you create a perfectly balanced cocktail every time. It looks like two cones connected at their narrowest part, opposite each other. Usually, one side holds 1½ ounces and the other ¾ ounce.

## *Paring Knife*

The paring knife will help you cut fruit easily. You probably already have one in your house. To make the perfect lemon garnish, cut a ½-by-1-inch slice off the rind and carefully avoid getting atoo much of the pith (the white part). With the skin side facing the drink, pinch assertively and quickly. You'll see the essence spray into the glass if you've done it right. Again, in my classes, it takes only twenty minutes or so for students to get the hang of cutting the perfect lemon or lime garnish. My Web site demonstrates how to do it.

*Bar Spoon*

*Bar spoon*

This is what gets tricky for new cocktail makers. The cocktail spoon is a long metal spoon, often sold with a twisted shaft. It's difficult to describe great bar spoon technique; it's a bit like trying to explain on paper how to use chopsticks or fold a napkin into a swan. It might take a little time to get the hang of it. If you don't feel like learning that skill, then don't. I'm fine with your stirring your drink without perfect technique as long as you don't "fist the shaft." That really does look silly.

I also stock different sizes of ice trays that I've found in kitchen stores. I like the look of one large ice globe floating in my old-fashioned or whiskey. Stacking small, perfectly square cubes into a tall Collins is a simple way to elevate the look of a cocktail without doing much else.

## CLASSIC WHISKEY COCKTAILS

We call these classic cocktails because they've been pleasing imbibers for a long time—in some instances for more than 150 years. Mastering the whiskey classic cocktails provides you with a base to start getting creative, too. Think of it like this: An artist often masters the drawing before creating abstractions, like Picasso. The balance, symmetry, and fundamentals of composition equip an artist with skills for success. Luckily, achieving finesse and beauty with a cocktail does not require Picasso-style dedication. You can have fun playing with acid, sweet, and bitters to find balance. And whiskey cocktails are also great with exotic ingredients, fresh seasonal fruits, and various kinds of sugars. For further reading, you can't go wrong purchasing a copy of *The PDT Cocktail Book* by Jim Meehan, which is a whopping three hundred pages of cocktail magic, complete with cool cartoon-y graphics. Until then, let me summarize for you the fundamentals, a Cocktails 101, if you will.

## Ingredients

1. Mixed drinks are made with at least two ingredients. A whiskey-soda, therefore, is a proper cocktail (see The Japanese Highball, page 138). After that, the sky's the limit, although you'll see most great cocktails hovering around the three- to four-ingredient mark.

2. You'll need what is called a "base spirit." In our little world here, that means whiskey. But other base spirits often include the obvious vodka, gin, rum, and tequila.

3. Sometimes, a "supporting role" spirit debuts—and for whiskey, the supporting role award goes to vermouth. Like vermouth used in a Manhattan, most secondary spirits contain less ABV and are used in smaller amounts. You should have no problem locating vermouth in your liquor store. There are sweet and dry styles and they can be fun to experiment with.

4. I think good cocktails need an acidic component, often offered up by a lemon or lime. But my bartender friends at The Flatiron Room created a killer cocktail with a large, juicy blood orange garnish that creates bar buzz every time it's served.

5. To balance the citrus and whiskey, a little sweetness is needed. Agave nectar, simple syrup, sweet vermouth (doing double duty), maple syrup, Demerara sugar, and molasses have all made appearances in my cocktails. For the most part, though, simple syrup will do.

6. Bitters! Don't be put off by that word. "But I don't like a bitter taste!" I've heard budding cocktail makers say in every class I've taught. They think using bitters leads to a bitter cocktail. Not so. Bitters add a complexity and depth to cocktails, much like salt does to food. Without a dash of bitters, the cocktail gods can't extol your mad skills.

7. Garnish. Garnish prepares us for what's inside the glass both aromatically and visually. I've draped maple-dipped fresh Vermont red currants over the side of a whiskey cocktail and I've perfected my own way to cut the rind off citrus, which takes about twenty minutes and five lemons to learn. Nose a bit of vanilla in that whiskey? Hint: might make a cool garnish. We'll talk more about "echoed flavor" in the food pairing chapter, but using garnish to bring out more of an exciting aroma can heighten a whiskey-drinking experience.

## Assembling

There are two ways to assemble your cocktail:

1. **Building:** You'll build the ingredients on top of one another in the glass. An old-fashioned is built right into the glass and stirred.
2. **Mixing:** "Mixed cocktails" means you'll add ingredients to a shaker, shake them, and strain them into a glass. A whiskey sour is a drink best served all shook up.

### SIMPLE SYRUP PRIMER

Many recipes in this book and elsewhere call for simple syrup, a solution made by dissolving sugar crystals in hot water. Hot water acts as a solvent for sugar, and when that water cools, careful measures of the syrup will harmoniously sweeten your cocktail. There's no comparing homemade simple syrup to a store-bought version. I find store-bought tastes cloyingly sweet and artificial. Once you get the hang of whizzing through the recipes below, which are used in the cocktails in this book, you can start experimenting with an endless combination of herbs and spices to create your own fantastic recipes.

To cool your syrup quickly, you can immerse a container of it in an ice bath and stir until cooled. Store your syrups in sealed jars in the refrigerator.

## SIMPLE SYRUP

Boil 1 part sugar and 1 part water in a pan. Simmer for 3 minutes. Cool.

For brown simple syrup, use brown sugar.

## THYME SYRUP

Boil 1 cup of water and 1 cup of sugar with two sprigs of thyme. Simmer for 3 minutes. Pour into a jar, cover, and let stand at room temperature overnight. Strain out the thyme before use.

## BEER STOUT SYRUP

Boil 1 cup of stout beer and 1 cup of sugar. Simmer for 1 minute. Cool.

## HONEY WATER

Heat equal parts honey and hot water. It's not necessary to boil honey. Cool.

## HONEY GINGER SYRUP

Boil 1 part ginger juice and 1 part honey. Simmer for 3 minutes. Cool before using.

To make ginger juice, juice your ginger in a juicer or blend ginger in a blender with a splash of water and then squeeze through a cheesecloth, which you can find in kitchen and grocery stores.

## CLASSIC COCKTAIL RECIPES

### WHISKEY SOUR

"Beauty of whatever kind, in its supreme development, invariably excites the sensitive soul to tears," wrote Edgar Allan Poe, who supposedly whacked himself out with a bottle of whiskey while yelling at himself in the mirror. It was a sad and fitting end to a rather macabre life he spent joined at the hip with my favorite spirit. He may have begun enjoying whiskey sours as a member of the Jefferson Literary and Debating Society, one of the oldest continually running collegiate debating societies, during his semester at the University of Virginia. Since 1825, every Friday night at 7:29, students gather with whiskey sours in hand to wax erudite on various topics. I suggest you gather your friends together and do the same. And in the spirit of dear Mr. Poe, be supreme in your whiskey sour development. Bring your friends to tears, but leave the bottle on the shelf.

**2 ounces bourbon or rye whiskey**
**½ ounce simple syrup**
**¾ ounce fresh lemon juice**
**½ ounce egg white (optional; gives the cocktail a frothy texture)**

Place the whiskey, simple syrup, lemon juice, and ice in a shaker and shake vigorously. If you are using egg white, first shake the ingredients together without the ice to emulsify the egg white. This is called a dry shake. Strain into your chosen whiskey sour glass. Garnish with an orange slice and a dark cherry.

### OLD-FASHIONED

Recipes for old-fashioneds vary as much as scrambled egg recipes do. Sports bar versions often come with a sweet and muddled gloop of maraschino cherries, orange slices, and cheap American whiskey, finished with a fine spray of "eau-de-bar-gun seltzer"—soda gun water tinged with Diet Coke remnants. That roller-rink version is my favorite when served alongside jalapeño peppers, wings, and cheese fries. If you want something more refined, however, I offer up this recipe, which will probably impress your friends more. They both follow the "old-fashioned" architecture of using bitters, sugar, whiskey, and ice in some order and in varying measures. Because this drink has been around since the late 1800s and in many forms, feel free to mess around to find your own style.

**Sugar cube**
**3 to 4 dashes Angostura bitters**
**Splash club soda (to dissolve the sugar)**
**2 ounces bourbon whiskey**

Put the sugar cube in the bottom of the glass. Cover with the bitters and splash of soda. Muddle with a muddler or spoon until you get a pretty good paste. Add ice, then the rye. Stir with a bar spoon for about 20 seconds to get all the ingredients in balance. Bartender Alex Valencia, who works at The Flatiron Room, counts to fifty and swears by that. Pinch a ½-inch slice of orange peel, with a snap and swiftness, skin side facing the glass, so that the orange oil sprays from the zest into the drink. Drop the zest into the drink and serve.

# MANHATTAN

My friend Jim Hewes, who tends bar and manages the whiskey list at The Willard InterContinental in Washington, D.C., is full of secret stories about who drinks what in the Washington scene. He'll never name names, or reveal too much, but you know that there is an exciting undercurrent of wheeling and dealing going all the time, which makes a trip to his bar worth every second of travel. He's got drinks up his sleeve for every president, and serves them during inaugural events.

The Manhattan, enjoyed with two cherries, was President William Howard Taft's favorite cocktail; it was probably made with rye, which is my favorite kind of whiskey to use for this treat. Rye's spice and high proof cut right through the cocktail, which is luxuriously balanced by a good vermouth and bitters. CEOs reading this should steer away from drinking Manhattans while doing your taxes—Taft was the first to impose a corporate income tax; therefore drinking one at the same time is basically a salute to him.

> **2 ounces bourbon or rye whiskey**
> **½ ounce sweet Italian vermouth**
> **3 to 4 dashes Angostura bitters**

Place the rye, vermouth, and bitters in a shaker and add ice. Stir with a bar spoon, blending together all the ingredients. Strain over a cocktail glass and garnish with a cherry or orange zest. By the way, a Manhattan made with Scotch is called a Rob Roy.

# MINT JULEP

This is the quintessential whiskey drink for the nonwhiskey drinker. Literally hundreds of "I don't like whiskey" guests at our bar have said, "This is good! Really good," after tasting a well-made julep. Of course, non-Yanks have been drinking this minty delight since at least 1803 when the description "a dram of spirituous liquor that has mint steeped in it, taken by Virginians of a morning" appeared in print in British traveler John Davis's book *Travels of Four Years and a Half in the United States of America*. Serve mint juleps in pewter julep cups with fresh mint, American bourbon, brown sugar, and crushed ice. Here's how I make them, a variation on the classic, which did not originally include lemon:

> **½ ounce simple syrup**
> **¾ ounce fresh lemon juice**
> **Handful fresh mint leaves**
> **2 ounces bourbon whiskey**

In a julep cup, place the syrup, lemon, and mint. Gently muddle the ingredients. Add the bourbon and crushed ice. Stir slightly, and garnish with a mint sprig and straw. Hint: I slap the mint between my two hands before garnishing. This little trick releases more aromatics from the leaves.

## BLOOD AND SAND

Big Scotch companies looking for a way to appeal to new whiskey drinkers started using various recipes of the Blood and Sand cocktail all over in bars in major cities around 2007, when the mixology craze was in full swing and the growth of premium Scotch looked endlessly promising. Tasting flights and paired whiskey dinners would begin with a Blood and Sand cocktail, served on trays either on ice or in a martini glass, strained. I think the reason for the resurgence of this classic was twofold: 1. It's hard to mess up this cocktail—it's a blend of four ingredients in equal parts, shaken. 2. It tastes equally good with Speyside, Highland, Lowland, or blended Scotches.

Named after a Rudolph Valentino movie of the same name, the color of the drink reflects the theme of the film, a slightly murky and smoky-looking maroon. You can prebatch these easily in large glass pitchers and shake individually when the time comes. Toast to the star known as the "Latin Lover" or, if you are lucky, to your own. Don't be put off by the disparate set of ingredients, either—the flavors pull together seamlessly.

1 part Scotch
1 part fresh orange juice
1 part cherry heering
1 part sweet Italian vermouth

Place the Scotch, orange juice, cherry heering, and vermouth in a shaker with ice and shake vigorously. Serve on the rocks or strain into a martini-style glass. Garnish with an orange peel or orange slice.

## NOVEL WHISKEY COCKTAILS

I've lost count of how many whiskey connoisseurs tell me that mixing whiskey into a cocktail ruins the spirit. I hope you see the folly in that philosophy by now. The bartenders at The Flatiron Room and I have spent the last year and a half focusing on whiskey cocktail creation with different varieties from around the world. We've played with hundreds of whiskeys. We are amazed by how a whiskey's flavor can dramatically change the aromatics, flavor, and drinking experience of a particular cocktail, even when all the other ingredients remain the same. My two partners in crime for the creation of the whiskey cocktails in this book—Alex Valencia and Hemant Pathak—came up with some stellar creations on a nightly basis. Our rule? Every cocktail must be based specifically on the aromatics and flavors found in whiskeys that can be purchased easily in the United States.

Cocktail making is personal, and night after night, Hemant and Alex offered me a sneak peek into their boyhoods through their drinks. The drinks were a celebration of exotic and faraway places like Uttar Pradesh, India, and Jalisco, Mexico. Hemant's cocktails displayed rich spices like cardamom and Darjeeling tea. Alex, who once told me that he jumps out of bed in the middle of the night to make drink recipes so that he doesn't forget them, creates bold and colorful cocktails, playing off the smoke in whiskeys and with available fruit. No doubt, he honed this skill while growing up around mescal and tequila, his hometown celebrities. His 37 West 26 cocktail, a balance of slight smoke, fig, and citrus, is one of the top sellers at The Flatiron Room. Coconut, one of the main aromatics found in hundreds of bourbons, is abundant in both Mexico and India, making my partners experts in bourbon cocktail making.

## ROUND (BAR) TABLE WITH HEMANT AND ALEX, WHISKEY COCKTAIL GURUS

**ME:** You two have wildly different approaches to your cocktails, and whenever you work the bar is crowded. How did it all begin? What made you fall in love with the craft?

**HEMANT:** For me, it was the simple and elegant idea that

elements of sweet, sour, and spirit are the building blocks for so many great cocktails. In India, my first taste was a rum drink called a daiquiri. It's simple, but perfect. Once you know how to balance those three S's you can create so many other drinks. For example, if you keep the sweet and sour elements of a daiquiri constant but change the spirit to bourbon, you have a whiskey sour. Change the spirit to tequila and it's now a margarita.

**ALEX:** I was nine and I loved drinking the sangrita—sort of a virgin Bloody Mary. I remember our neighbors made it with tomato juice, spices, hot sauce, and cucumber juice. Later I drank it with tequila—called a vampirito. I wanted to make drinks like that.

**ME:** How do you think these childhood memories from your home countries influence your cocktail making?

**ALEX:** I developed a savory and spicy palate at a very young age, so now working with whiskey as an ingredient comes naturally to me. Guadalajara, where I grew up, is famous for savory and spicy food: *tacos de birra, tortas ahogadas, ceviche,* and tequila. Our margaritas are world famous, too, so when I started making drinks, I wanted to please the Mexican palate around me. I remember parties where each food was tied to its specialist: one guy made *ceviche* and another made *tortas ahogadas.* Those guys were always famous for what they did, were appreciated in the community, and treated with respect. I want to be known as the guy who makes awesome drinks for you.

**HEMANT:** Most of my classic twists on cocktails are based on the Asian and Indian herbs and spices I grew up with. My first introduction to spices was through my mom as she cooked. She taught me how to get balance with herbs and spices. At that time, I didn't know her lessons would be my best friends throughout my career.

**ME:** Let's talk about bar etiquette. A lot of customers tell me they feel intimidated at a bar, especially a whiskey bar such as ours. Any advice?

**HEMANT:** It's okay to say, "Surprise me!" at a nice bar. I like it when a guest challenges me by giving me some flavor guidelines. This is a great way to come up with new cocktails, too.

**ALEX:** It's not required, but it is nice when a regular customer remembers my name, I remember theirs, and we have a good conversation. Don't be shy to chat with us. It's those little things that make a great bar vibe.

**ME:** Is an American audience different from the one from which you came? How?

**HEMANT:** In America, there are tons of liquor brands available, which allows the home bartender to be a "cocktailian" if they want to. Americans are also ahead of other countries in terms of cocktail options at the bar. They have more advanced bar palates.

**ALEX:** Also, Americans are able to spend more than people can back in Mexico. This allows them to experiment with all the different spirits, wines, and cuisines that are available to them. American chefs, sommeliers, and bartenders here have the biggest opportunity to develop their art—even the home bartender can, too. There is just so much here.

**ME:** What are the aromatics in a whiskey you love most to play with?

**HEMANT:** The best thing I like in whiskey is peat—it's so fun to play with. I also like to identify the fruits and spices in a whiskey, and balance or enhance these flavors with additional Indian or Asian ingredients.

**ALEX:** For me, that depends on my mood and the season. I like to play off the spice in whiskey when it's really cold outside. I look for bourbon with loads of vanilla and coconut during the summer months. Japanese whisky is versatile; I like the dry fruit aromas the wood gives to a Japanese whisky. Even the smell of corn on a young and rustic whiskey is fun to play with if I'm in that sort of mood.

**ME:** What is your best advice for a budding home bartender?

**ALEX:** Believe in your palate! Don't buy a spirit just because you saw it on television. When you can, support small or craft spirits. The expensive spirit will not always be best—there are wonderful options at good prices.

**HEMANT:** Nothing is more perfect than a cocktail that exceeds your guests' expectations—even if it is simple! Get the best, freshest ingredients possible. But most of all, be a good host, make guests feel important and welcome. A quality drink combined with great hospitality leads to a quality drinking experience, even if it's a well-done but very simple drink.

Here are our original whiskey creations. I've included a difficulty level so you can have a sense of it before you get started. Many of these are perfect for a quick everyday drink—and they'll all please a crowd.

## Original Recipes

## 37 WEST 26

Whiskey: Johnnie Walker Black, Amrut Fusion, Bowmore 12
Creator: Alex Valencia
Level: Moderate
Flavor Profile: Slightly smoky and rich, with a light citrus top note, which makes the drink a little mysterious yet approachable. Imagine drinking this while watching Lauren Bacall in *Dark Passage.*

> **2 dry figs**
> **½ ounce simple syrup**
> **¾ ounce fresh lemon juice**
> **2 to 4 dashes Peychaud's bitters**
> **½ ounce Drambuie**
> **2 ounces whiskey**

Muddle the figs in a shaker with the simple syrup. Add the lemon juice, bitters, Drambuie, and whiskey and ice. Shake vigorously. Strain and serve on the rocks. Garnish with lemon peel squeezed for oils and an open fig and lemon round.

### MASTER THE MUDDLE

Muddling is very easy to do: Place herbs and fruit in the bottom of a sturdy glass, and gently press down on the ingredients while turning slightly with a tool called a muddler (it looks like a small wooden bat). The end of a wooden spoon works, too. Don't press and turn aggressively, though; you don't want to shred the leaves and release bitter chlorophyll into your cocktail. Add ice only after you've muddled. If you add it beforehand, it will shred your ingredients. As you muddle, mint, basil, raspberry, and other luscious aromatics (depending on the recipe) will start wafting toward your nose, and that's your clue you've muddled just enough.

# KILIMANJARO

Whiskey: Glenfiddich 12, Compass Box's Great King Street, Knappogue Castle 12
Creator: Author
Level: Easy
Flavor Profile: Refreshing, zesty, and thirst quenching. Think backyard picnic, or an outdoor patio bar while on safari in Africa. In fact, I made this cocktail after I had just finished climbing Kilimanjaro in Africa. We were celebrating at a local bar in Arusha, and the barkeep asked, "Would you make a whiskey cocktail for us?" There were scant ingredients, but I managed to build a drink using the pear-forward Glenfiddich and some seriously spicy ginger beer made in Tanzania. Later, I added fresh lavender to enhance some of Glenfiddich's floral notes, along with the pear and ginger. Great King Street and Knappogue Castle 12 are two other whiskeys with notes of green apple and pear, and can be used harmoniously in this drink as well.

**2 ounces whiskey**
**Fresh ginger beer**
**6 dashes Peychaud's bitters**

Pour the whiskey into the bottom of a glass. Add ice and the ginger beer, and top with the bitters until a light rose color is reached. Garnish with a fresh lavender flower, if you like.

# FOOL'S GOLD

Whiskey: Glenmorangie Nectar D'or, Yamazaki 12, Compass Box Great King Street
Creator: Alex Valencia
Level: Easy
Flavor Profile: Colorful, fruit forward, and floral. A Victorian-era heroine would drink this quietly in her bedroom before descending for dinner. I love using the Sauternes cask–finished Glenmorangie Nectar D'or for this cocktail. The whisky's complexity keeps this cocktail from being too cloying. Both Yamazaki and Great King Street are good options with their light, floral, and crisp notes, too. You can garnish this with edible flowers to highlight the heather, honey, fruity, and green notes of the whiskeys.

> **3 fresh raspberries, muddled**
> **½ ounce simple syrup**
> **¾ ounce fresh lemon juice**
> **2 ounces Glenmorangie Nectar D'or**

Place the raspberries, simple syrup, lemon juice, and whiskey in a shaker and shake vigorously. Strain and serve up in a martini glass. Garnish with raspberries or edible flowers or even a rose.

# LIME THYME SOUR

Whiskey: Bulleit Bourbon, Basil Hayden, Four Roses Yellow Label (these high-rye bourbons, each with its own unique notes, work well in this cocktail)
Creator: Hemant Pathak
Level: Difficult
Flavor Profile: Slightly spicy, earthy, herbal, and acidic with that autumn pie smell of the bourbon. Serve during late September, with the last of the remaining summer light and fresh herbs.

> **2 ounces bourbon whiskey**
> **½ ounce homemade thyme syrup**
> **¾ ounce fresh lime juice**

Place the whiskey, thyme syrup, and lime juice in a shaker with ice and shake vigorously. Strain into a martini or other coupe glass and garnish with a layer of thyme foam (below).

## WINE, LIME, AND THYME FOAM

**4 egg whites**
**4 ounces sauvignon blanc white wine**
**¾ ounce homemade thyme syrup**
**1 ounce fresh lime juice**

Put the egg whites, white wine, thyme syrup, and lime juice in a nitrogen charger (also called a soda selzer siphon), shake, and charge foam onto the drink to top it off. Garnish with a sprig of thyme.

## TENDRIL COCKTAIL

Whiskey: Maker's Mark, Larceny, Rebel Yell, or other wheated bourbon
Creator: Hemant Pathak
Level: Moderate
Flavor Profile: Light, fresh, and green. This is a whiskey cocktail you could drink in the tropics and even in a champagne glass during a warm summer evening.

**½ fresh kiwifruit**
**1 small blade lemongrass**
**½ ounce Monin caramel simple syrup**
**¾ ounce fresh lemon juice**
**2 ounces wheated bourbon**

Muddle kiwi and lemongrass with the caramel syrup. Add the lemon juice, bourbon, and ice; shake well. Strain and serve into a martini or champagne flute; garnish with a fresh kiwi slice and lemongrass.

# GREEN GLORY FIZZ

Whiskey: The Balvenie 12 DoubleWood, GlenDronach 12, Dalmore 12
Creator: Hemant Pathak
Level: Moderate
Flavor Profile: Slightly sweet, a bit spicy, and with a perfect amount of acid, all pulled together as they should be. The star anise gives this a slightly exotic nose while the egg white gives a nice meringuelike texture. Honey, caramel, and spice are notes found in the Balvenie 12 DoubleWood, GlenDronach 12, and Dalmore 12. Echoed flavors found in the honey ginger syrup enhance the style of whiskeys used.

   **2 ounces whiskey**
   **½ ounce honey ginger syrup**
   **1 slice orange peel (approximately 1 by ½ inch)**
   **¾ ounce egg white**
   **¾ ounce freshly squeezed lemon juice**
   **Splash seltzer water**

Place the whiskey, honey ginger syrup, orange peel, egg whites, and lemon juice in a shaker and dry shake (without ice to emulsify the egg white), add ice and shake again. Strain into a tall glass and top off with a splash of seltzer water. Garnish with star anise, lemon peel, or both.

# FRENCH CONNECTION

Whiskey: Brenne
Creator: Hemant Pathak
Level: Moderate
Flavor Profile: Tropical, lush, with loads of banana, vanilla, raisin, and cherry. This makes a fabulous aperitif, served chilled in a dessert-style wineglass.

   **1½ ounces Brenne**
   **½ ounce dry vermouth**

½ ounce grand banana liquor (cognac, white crème de cacao, banana syrup)

Stir together the Brenne, vermouth, grand banana liquor, and ice in a mixing glass. Strain the ingredients into a small dessert wine coupe. Garnish with any of the notes you might find in this very unique whiskey: banana, lemongrass, or macerated cherries, for example.

## DIY BANANA LIQUOR

Bananas are notoriously tough to work with—they are fibrous and mushy. So how can we get that nice rich banana hint in a whiskey laden with aromatics like coconut, almonds, cherries, or even banana itself? For the adventurous, give this a try.

1 part cognac
½ part white crème de cacao
½ part Monin banana syrup

Put the cognac, crème de cacao, and banana syrup in a mixing glass and mix by simply stirring with a spoon.

## CANADIAN SNEAK

Whiskey: WhistlePig Rye from Vermont, which is currently made with rye casks from Canada; High West Rendezvous Rye; or Rittenhouse Rye
Creator: Author
Level: Easy
Flavor Profile: Maple, nutty, spicy, and slightly sweet. Make after raking leaves, especially.

2 ounces whiskey
¾ ounce fresh lemon juice
½ ounce maple syrup
4 dashes Angostura bitters

**2 pinches ground cinnamon (I prefer a little more; experiment with your own tastes)**

Combine the whiskey, lemon juice, maple syrup, bitters, and cinnamon in a shaker and shake vigorously. Strain and pour into a rocks glass filled with ice. Garnish with a cinnamon stick and lemon slice, or maple-dipped red currants. Sprinkle the top with cinnamon.

# AUTUMN POET

Whiskey: Michter's Bourbon, Angel's Envy Bourbon
Creator: Alex Valencia
Level: Easy
Flavor Profile: Full-bodied cocktail with deep cherry, chocolate almond, and vanilla notes. This cocktail takes advantage of both Michter's and Angel's Envy's sexy richness. This is a year-round cocktail.

**2 ounces bourbon whiskey**
**¾ ounce fresh lemon juice**
**½ ounce simple syrup**
**½ ounce grenadine syrup**
**Dash absinthe**

Place the bourbon, lemon juice, simple syrup, and grenadine syrup in a shaker and shake vigorously. Strain into a martini glass. Garnish with a cherry or blueberries, which complement the dark fruits in Michter's Bourbon.

# ADDIE GRAHAM

Whiskey: A classic bourbon such as Knob Creek, Buffalo Trace, or Wild Turkey
Creator: Alex Valencia

Level: Easy
Flavor Profile: Fresh, green, minty, and sweet; a cross between a mojito and a mint julep but with a fresh basil tinge. Serve outside during the warm months.

> ½ **lemon, cut into 4 pieces**
> **4 to 6 fresh basil leaves**
> ¾ **ounce brown simple syrup**
> **2 ounces bourbon whiskey**

Muddle in a shaker the lemon and basil leaves. Add the simple syrup and bourbon to the lemon. Shake all the ingredients with ice only for 5 seconds so as not to shred the basil leaves. Strain into a tall glass and serve over crushed ice with a straw. Garnish with more fresh basil.

# SCOTTISH CHAI

Whiskey: Oban, Talisker, Johnnie Walker Gold Reserve, Amrut Fusion
Creator: Hemant Pathak
Level: Difficult
Flavor Profile: Black tea, Indian spices, herbs, smoke, and peat. Sip this cocktail while watching three oceans converge in southern India, or at least imagine you are there.

> 1½ **ounces Darjeeling tea**
> **2 ounces whiskey**
> ¼ **ounce dry vermouth**
> ¼ **ounce peach liqueur**
> ½ **ounce honey water (see page 193)**
> **1 dash Angostura Orange Bitters**

Brew the tea and wait for it to cool. In a mixing glass, stir in the tea, whiskey, vermouth, peach liqueur, and honey water and ice together. Strain into a martini glass and garnish with a bourbon-infused spiced cherry.

## ADD SOME CHERRY CHIC TO YOUR COCKTAIL

You can use bourbon and spice-infused cherries for your Manhattan-style cocktails and the Scottish Chai Cocktail in this book to elevate your cocktails to darn near art. Here's how to make them!

**HEMANT'S BOURBON-SPICED CHERRIES**

1 cup black cherries

2 star anise

1 cinnamon stick

5 cloves

6 cardamom beans

Pinch saffron

1 cup bourbon

Put the cherries, star anise, cinnamon, cloves, cardamom, saffron, and bourbon in an airtight jar and let it sit overnight, being careful not to expose the infusing ingredients to direct sunlight. Strain the spices. You can leave the cherries and the bourbon stored in a jar in the refrigerator. Use within 1 week.

# PATHAK'S PUNCH

"Punch" means "five" in Hindi, and, indeed, five things make a perfect punch: something sweet, something sour, a spirit, juice (or cordial), and water.

Whiskey: Glenmorangie 10, Yamazaki 12, Auchentoshan Three Wood

Creator: Hemant Pathak

Level: Medium

Flavor Profile: Reminiscent of a mango lassi. Slightly thicker in texture, this cocktail delivers tropical mango notes balanced with a slight spicy nuttiness found in both the sherry and the stout. I imagine drinking this cool rich concoction in lieu of a piña colada while swinging on a hammock.

> 2 ounces whiskey
> 1 ounce mango puree
> ½ ounce beer stout syrup
> ¾ ounce fresh lemon juice

Put the whiskey, mango puree, beer stout syrup, and lemon juice in a shaker with ice, shake vigorously, and strain into an all-purpose wineglass. Garnish with a slice of mango and a pinch of allspice powder.

# 6

## Whiskey and Food

*Pairings for Every Occasion*

YES, YOU CAN PAIR food with whiskey! I drink whiskey with lots of different dishes, and I sip them alongside my appetizer, entrée, or dessert the same way you already do with your favorite wine. The first step when you are thinking about pairing is to consider the weather, time of day, cuisine, your mood, the context, and the person you are sharing your time with—like food, *whiskey is about occasion.* For this simple reason, I am never able to effectively answer, "What's your favorite whiskey?" And if you ask me, "What's your deserted island whiskey?" I'll return with a few questions of my own: Will I have access to ice? Who is with me? Is the island Greenland? The Seychelles?

Imagine this: It's early March and the promise of spring is just around the corner, but the brutal chill of February still nags you. A dusting of snow covers a few of the trees that begin to poke a few buds. It's gray and damp, the window is open a slight crack—just enough for a bit of fresh air. I call this easy whiskey, Irish stew weather: You sink your teeth into soft braised meats, potatoes, and vegetables cooked together in a big pot alongside the season's last fire in the fireplace. You pour yourself and your partner a glass of creamy Irish whiskey with notes of spring: grass, fruits, and a hint of florals. All the herbs, vegetables, meats, and broth pair perfectly with the green and slight floral elements of an Irish whiskey.

On the other hand, a bad breakup calls for something big, American, and tough. A two-finger pour of spicy rye with some cheap bar food with your pals is the perfect antidote to a crappy day and a bad fight. Have a couple of friends popping by last minute? I like to pull together a chic and easy spread: Scotch poured into some killer vintage glassware alongside a marble or wood slab covered in a variety of charcuterie and cheeses.

So, whiskey and food pairings can often come down to intuition of taste. I won't leave you out on a limb though, aimlessly wandering the whiskey aisle without some more guidance. There are some key guidelines I'm going to give to you, based on years of belly-busting experiments and my whiskey-fanatic executive chef-pal Rob Bleifer's golden rules: *"First, be aware of acidity and fats in your food. Then, think about this: Pair like flavors to make flavors echo, pair complementing flavors to bring out a bigger picture, or pair contrasting flavors to allow them to duke it out."*

I hear you, foodies—you're mumbling to yourselves that that's pretty obvious advice. But whiskey is a wild little beverage, and I'm only just now nailing some killer food and whiskey pairings after years of tasting and sampling. I'll share my best-bet food-pairing chart along with what I call whiskey "flavor friends" at the end of this chapter so that you can flavor-match your whiskey like a pro.

## TENET NUMBER ONE: PAIR LIKE FLAVORS TO MAKE FLAVORS ECHO

Pecan pie and Kentucky bourbon. Smoked salmon with Islay whisky. Dark chocolate pot de crème with spicy rye. These simple, crowd-pleasing pairings will get your neighbors enviously whispering to one another that they wish they'd thought to serve such sensory delights instead of a white wine and Cracker Barrel cheese. What makes these pairings click? Because they fall under Rob's first tenet: They share some of the same flavors. In other words, they echo each other. Bourbon, bursting with vanillas and spice, echoes ingredients baked into homemade American pies like pecan, sweet potato, and pumpkin. Rye whiskeys that deliver hints of chocolate with a slightly dry and tannic note echo the slight bitterness of a dark chocolate pot de crème. Smoky whiskeys and smoked fish is always a winning combination, especially when the fish is served with a dollop of fat, like crème fraîche or butter (more on fats later). Try thin slices of smoked salmon on thin baguette slices with a dab of crème fraîche on top, served with a carefully chosen Scotch.

Once you've identified your favorite styles of whiskeys and their flavors, look for foods with similar flavors to pair with them. Create your own meals by cooking with ingredients that mimic the ones found in your favorite whiskey.

## TENET NUMBER TWO: COMPLEMENTARY FLAVORS BRING ABOUT A "BIGGER PICTURE"

In order to get really slick at combining complementing flavors, choose your favorite whiskey and write down three aromatics you love about the particular bottle. Let's say you picked The Balvenie 12 DoubleWood and that you've identified notes of orange, honey, and some spice. You'll then hit the grocery or peruse a food menu and look for any items that taste good with those particular notes, but don't actually *contain or echo* the same notes. For example, what sorts of ingredients pair well with honey? Here are a few: duck, chicken, almonds, cheese, chocolate, ice cream, lavender, and ginger. Could a roast duck with ginger pair well with my whiskey? I would think so—I'd order that off the Chinese takeout menu based on the aromatics I've identified in my favorite whiskey. And if you're a chef? Add the echoed flavor of orange and honey to your duck and ginger dish to enhance both complementary and echoed flavors.

For me, the orange aromatic in The Balvenie pairs tastefully with some dark chocolate. Not only do they have complementary tastes, but the combination triggers a shared memory for me. My mother always put an orange in my Christmas stocking along with loads of chocolate, and I'd eat them both Christmas morning before eating breakfast. I also like some Balvenie 12 with almonds, ice cream, and some lavender-infused honey drizzled on top. I think you get the idea—and that is to get creative and play a little bit.

## TENET NUMBER THREE: PAIR CONTRASTING FLAVORS TO DUKE IT OUT

I dump M&Ms in movie popcorn and I can't stop eating it. That salty versus sweet thing going on in my mouth could keep me going for a very long time. That's also why salted caramel chocolates have become so popular lately—haven't you seen them around a lot more? The effect of these opposite tastes duking it out creates a richer, more exciting gustatory experience. I look for the same excitement in my whiskey pairings.

Salty, cured meats bring out the sweetness in whiskey, which makes charcuterie a nice pairing with whiskey. Salt also reduces the bitter sensation, so mouth-puckering, tannic qualities found in some whiskeys will reveal as more velvety when paired with salted foods. Try a trifecta of contrasting, echoed, and complementary ingredients by drinking sweet bourbon with slices of salty, caramelized ham slices layered on a fatty biscuit and drizzled with a bit of maple syrup.

### CHOCOLATE AND WHISKEY: GO FOR IT!

Once I went on a two-week chocolate and whiskey binge trying to uncover some perfect pairings for a class. I went through a lot of chocolate and one hundred types of whiskey—and here's the bottom line: Chocolate and whiskey almost always work together, no matter what the whiskey or chocolate. What changes are the flavor sensations—for example, milk chocolate makes very sweet American whiskeys taste a bit drier and more balanced because your palate adapts to the sweetness (adaptive tasting), while salted caramel chocolate will make a dry tannic whiskey taste slightly less bitter on the tongue, because salt eases bitterness. If you swap the pairings, you'll have a different experience, but it will still be tasty. The possibilities are infinite.

## GREAT PAIRINGS

### Whiskey with Fatty Foods

Before the advent of all the new mixology and whiskey joints, steak houses were the only places I could find great whiskeys on a night out. This makes sense. From a purely physical perspective, the fats in meat will coat your mouth and, as a result, soften the alcohol on our receptors. A sip of whiskey then washes away those fats, acting like a palate cleanser, making us ready for more. It's that back-and-forth feeling of coating and cleansing that makes whiskey so wonderful with fats. Steaks, fish, chocolates, and cheeses are all foods that contain a good amount of fats that hold up to whiskey's high alcohol content. If you ask me, I could pretty much live on cheese, chocolate, and whiskey. (I try not to.)

Many years ago, I was asked to create a menu with a national steak house chain for a series of whiskey dinners across the United States. Our dinner menu included rib eye and a green salad with apples, pears, cheese, and a light citrus dressing. We chose the dressing to echo flavors of the young, nonpeated single malt Scotch we served. For dessert, we offered molten chocolate cake with vanilla custard to echo the flavors of a sherry-influenced single malt Scotch. The fats in all of the dishes mellowed whiskey's high alcohol content, and sauces that use berries echoed or complemented many whiskey notes. At The Flatiron Room, chef Susan Burdian serves braised short ribs covered in a spoonful of a warm bramble sauce over creamy polenta in little cast-iron pots. I recommend that dish with sherry-influenced single malt Scotches like GlenDronach or The Dalmore, which have dark-fruit notes like berries and figs.

## Be Careful with Acids and Spice

The high alcohol content in whiskeys also means that you should be careful with acidic foods like tomatoes—I haven't yet found a whiskey to enjoy alongside traditional Italian pastas, ratatouille, or Mexican dishes, for example. High acids and high alcoholic, wood-influenced spirits have an intensity that just doesn't really work with highly acidic foods like pasta with tomato sauce. Or at least the combination doesn't work for me. I can practically feel an ulcer developing in my stomach lining when I think about spicy salsa and bourbon digesting at the same time.

Another odd but interesting phenomenon is that whiskey paired with spicy foods will make that spicy food even spicier—and it's progressive. A hot pepper will taste even hotter with a whiskey, and after ten minutes of "enjoying" both, you'll be running red to the kitchen for milk and ice.

## When All Else Fails: What Grows Together, Goes Together

While there are always exceptions to the rule, I find that this rule is a great starting point for identifying easy pairings. When The Flatiron Room asked me to find a whiskey that I could pair with seitan tacos, lime, cabbage, and Japanese kabocha squash, I was stumped. After trying a bunch of bourbons and Scotches, one of the waiters said, "Why don't we go Japanese on this one?" He was right. The very lightly citrusy and floral Yamazaki 12 complemented the sweetness of the Japanese squash as if no other whiskey in the world was meant for it.

## AT-HOME FOOD SCIENCE EXPERIMENT— DEVELOP YOUR OWN BEST PAIRING!

1. Choose your favorite whiskey, be it bourbon, rye, or single malt, and pour a dram for yourself at your table.
2. Assemble the following ingredients: some pure sugar, salt, a piece of cheese, some vinegar, and a protein like chicken, steak, or fish, if you want to serve meats.
3. Take a sip of your whiskey.
4. After a few seconds, put some pure sugar on your finger or a spoon, and then put that in your mouth. Let it absorb onto your tongue, and then down your throat.
5. Take a sip of that same whiskey again.
6. Record what happened: Did the whiskey become bitter? Did it mellow out? Did the sugar enhance the flavor of the whiskey? Take away from the flavor?
7. Proceed through all the ingredients you've assembled this way—you will see how dynamic the whiskey becomes depending on the sugars, salts, acids, or fats you taste right beforehand. Now, go through the ingredients again, and this time taste the ingredient and the whiskey together. Do they complement each other? Duke it out? You'll begin to develop a rudimentary architecture . . . you can get even more complex by pulling out ice cream, a piece of pie, salted caramel chocolate, and so on.

8. Develop an appetizer or dinner menu based on your own observations about your favorite whiskey paired with the fundamental tastes in this experiment. Serve something sweet and fatty if you found that sweets and fat made your whiskey nice. If you found that vinegar didn't take away from the whiskey, then you know that a dressed salad would be okay.

9. Take pride in your ability to pull off a whiskey–food paired menu.

## TABLE 5: THE INCOMPLETE FOOD AND WHISKEY PAIRING CHART (BECAUSE YOU'LL DISCOVER MORE)

Based on principles I've talked about in this chapter, here are some go-to pairings that you can start to use immediately. But don't be afraid to use your own culinary skills and instincts to create more whiskey and food pairing gems on your own. You can also use this guide to find the best foods on restaurant menus to pair with whiskey.

| WHISKEY STYLE | POSSIBLE PROTEIN/ ENTRÉE MATCHES | CHEESE BOARD OPTIONS | DESSERT OPTIONS | LOOK FOR THESE INGREDIENTS OR FLAVOR PROFILES |
|---|---|---|---|---|
| Smoky, Peated Whiskeys | Smoked fish chowder<br>Salmon<br>Raw oysters<br>Steak (especially rib eye or strip) | Asiago<br>Roquefort<br>Stilton<br>Pecorino<br>Smoked Gouda<br>Morbier | | Bacon<br>Honey<br>Melon<br>Coffee |

| WHISKEY STYLE | POSSIBLE PROTEIN/ ENTRÉE MATCHES | CHEESE BOARD OPTIONS | DESSERT OPTIONS | LOOK FOR THESE INGREDIENTS OR FLAVOR PROFILES |
|---|---|---|---|---|
| Sherry-Influenced Scotch | Steak (especially rib eye or strip)<br>Roast beef<br>Duck<br>Pork<br>Lamb<br>Salmon | Cheddar<br>Gouda<br>Manchego<br>Pecorino | Crème brûlée<br>Bread pudding<br>Dried fruits<br>Ice cream<br>Fruitcake<br>Custards | Figs<br>Raisins<br>Toffee<br>Caramel<br>Walnuts<br>Bananas<br>Butterscotch<br>Prunes<br>Currants<br>Raspberries<br>Blackberries<br>Dates |
| Nonpeated, Nonsherried, Malted Barley–Based Whiskeys Aged in Refill Barrels | Lamb<br>Steak (especially rib eye or strip)<br>Short ribs<br>Duck<br>Pork<br>Dorade<br>Dover sole<br>Snapper<br>Tuna<br>Sushi<br>Indian curry<br>Chinese takeout<br>Sweet potatoes | Cheddar<br>Gouda<br>Manchego<br>Pecorino<br>Muenster | Dark chocolate<br>Custards<br>Ice cream<br>Shortbread | Ginger<br>Orange<br>Honey<br>Lemon<br>Pears<br>Walnuts<br>Anise<br>Lavender<br>Apples<br>Cranberries<br>Dates |

| WHISKEY STYLE | POSSIBLE PROTEIN/ ENTRÉE MATCHES | CHEESE BOARD OPTIONS | DESSERT OPTIONS | LOOK FOR THESE INGREDIENTS OR FLAVOR PROFILES |
|---|---|---|---|---|
| American Rye | Steak (especially rib eye or strip)<br>Roast beef<br>Short ribs<br>Bacon<br>Pork<br>BBQ (ribs, chicken, brisket)<br>Ham<br>Sweet potatoes | Cheddar<br>Gouda<br>Jack<br>Colby<br>Gruyère | Chocolate (milk, white, dark)<br>American pies (especially pecan, peach, sweet potato, pumpkin)<br>Doughnuts | Coconut<br>Vanilla<br>Almonds<br>Cherries<br>Maple<br>Cinnamon<br>Cranberries<br>Cloves<br>Orange zest |
| Bourbon | Steak (especially rib eye or strip)<br>Roast beef<br>Bacon<br>Pork<br>BBQ (ribs, brisket, chicken)<br>Scallops<br>Hamburgers<br>Ham<br>Sweet potatoes | Cheddar<br>Aged Gouda<br>Monterey Jack<br>P'tit Basque<br>Manchego<br>Colby | Chocolate (milk, white, dark)<br>American pies (especially pecan, peach, sweet potato, pumpkin)<br>Peaches<br>Doughnuts | Mint<br>Orange<br>Bacon<br>Almonds<br>Cherries<br>Cranberries<br>Orange blossom water<br>Vanilla<br>Peach<br>Apricots |

## TABLE 6: THE WHISKEY OCCASION CHART

The following chart includes some whiskey recommendations based on a number of whiskey-drinking conundrums, including what to drink at a rock concert and what to drink with Halloween candy. Since so many of you ask me what I drink on a regular basis, I thought I'd share some specifics.

| OCCASION | TOP WHISKEY PICKS | RATIONALE |
|---|---|---|
| Halloween | Cheap bourbon | Needs to pair with cheap milk chocolate |
| Hanukkah | www.kosherliquorlist.com | Blessed by rabbi |
| New Year's Eve | Whiskey highballs (see The Japanese Highball, page 138) | I want to keep going all night, not get tanked, and I want something sparkly. |
| Breakfast | American rye whiskey | It's 12:00 a.m. somewhere, and these whiskeys go with maple syrup and pancakes. |
| Business Lunch | Nonpeated, nonsherried, young Scotch | I want something light and on the rocks and I still need to get back to work. |
| Aperitif Hour | Brenne on the rocks with a slice of orange<br>Old-fashioned | I want to whet the appetite and not overwhelm it. |
| Bad Day | Jack Daniel's<br>Johnnie Walker Black | I want to hear the sound of the glass hitting the bar as I put it down, and I'm in no mood for anything precious. |
| Indie or Rock Concert | Maker's Mark<br>Johnnie Walker Black<br>Jack Daniel's | Usually the best music venue options |
| Summer Evening on the Beach | Glenmorangie Nectar D'or<br>Hakushu 12<br>Brenne | I want light, refreshing whiskey I can put on the rocks. |
| Best Gift for Someone Who Requires Some Flash | Anything Macallan<br>Johnnie Walker Blue<br>Pappy Van Winkle<br>Anything Balvenie | They taste good, and they have a wow factor for the image conscious. (But good luck finding the Pappy.) |

# Acknowledgments

WRITING A BOOK ON whiskey was harder than I thought it would be. Essentially, I had to learn how to write a book while I was writing a book. Crafting this acknowledgments page makes me nervous again. Who might I forget? How far back in time do I go? When does it get too extensive? I don't know the answer to those questions. My philosophy is that what I do every day is really a summation of my whole life, and that makes it hard to pinpoint when I started creating this book and where to start thanking. It wrote itself as I lived, going back to a binky dipped in whiskey and continuing forward to this moment, sitting in my favorite café. Come to think of it, my whiskey destiny was probably sealed the day I was born and named Heather, in honor of my Scottish grandpa, a flower, and a whiskey note. Scientists, chefs, writers, distilleries, artists, coworkers, friends, and family cheered me on to fulfill what I guess was written on stars for me.

I raise my glass to:

## THE SCIENTISTS

Dr. Leslie Stein and the rest of her team at the Monell Chemical Senses Center; Dr. Rachel Herz, world-renowned expert on the psychological science of smell; Renee Gonzales, PhD; and Dr. Rachel Barrie, Master Blender at Morrison-Bowmore Distillers. The work that you all do is nothing short of extraordinary. Special thanks to Nicole Austin, Master Blender, Kings County Distillery of Brooklyn, who provided a lot of technical information and even contributed to the book.

## THE WRITER-FRIEND CHEERLEADERS

Liza Weisstuck, Fred Minnick, Amy Zavatto, and Dave Wondrich; each of you is an inspiration to me and has somewhere along this journey been really helpful. Thanks. Michael Veach, Ken Simon, and Adam Robb, thank you for being readers on drafts of the book and wonderful people to boot. While I'm at it, I'm also going to thank Kara Newman for helping me to pull together my jumbled thoughts into a salable proposal. Jim Meehan, you shared that the secret of a solid cocktail chapter would be a strong point of view. Thank you for your input as I wrote this book.

## THE ARTISTS

I had no idea how many talented artists are needed to pull a book together. I count these skilled artisans among the best in the business: graphic designer Jennifer Muller, makeup artist Sally Duval, photographers Matt Wells and Steve Giralt, book designer Renato Stanisic, prop stylist Penelope Bouklas, and illustrator John Burgoyne. Thank you all tremendously. Toni Brogan, you get a special shout-out, because you held my hand through the whole thing and are without a doubt the best food stylist and art director working today. I'm glad you are my friend, too.

## THE FLATIRON ROOM TEAM

Tommy Tardie, you played a particularly important role during the year I wrote this book. Your generosity, encouraging words said to me every week, and the business I've watched you take to the top really inspires me. What you build people get behind. I am one of those people. Here are a couple of others on your team whom I'd like to thank: Chef Susan Burdian, Evelina Ioselev, David Garcia, Gina Garcia, and Lily Sato. You all make me laugh regularly (or feed me) and add such spice to my life.

## THE WILLIAM GRANT AND SONS GANG

Thanks Ian Millar: You never once used the adjective "female" before "whiskey expert." Thank you for believing in me. I will always cherish memories of traveling through Scotland with you. David Allardice, Mitch Bechard, Freddy May, Nicholas Polachhi, Sam Simmons, Andy Weir, Brian Kinsman, David Mair, David Stewart, Tim Herlihy, Julie Ettles, Joanne Jones, Collette Leonard, April Finklestein, David Bitran, Andy Nash, and Lindsay Prociw, thanks for making my time at William Grant and Sons so memorable.

## THE AMERICAN WHISKEY GANG

Tuthilltown, Wild Turkey, Kings County, Michter's, Catskills Distilling, Balcones, Buffalo Trace, Woodford Reserve, Widow Jane, Hillrock, Heaven Hill, and Angel's Envy—you have all been very hospitable to me. Stacy Yates and Susan Dallas of Louisville Tourism, you are as generous and elegant as I imagined women from Kentucky to be. Thank you.

## THE JAPANESE

Akiko Azuma, what a wonderful entrée you created for me into Japanese culture. Thank you for an unforgettable visit with you and your beautiful family. Thanks also to Yamazaki and Suntory distilleries, especially Mike Miyamoto, Gardner Dunn, and Neyha White for your hospitality and sharing your knowledge. Star Bar Ginza, I still dream about your highballs.

## AND THIS HODGEPODGE

Allison Patel, Melissa Caruso Scott, Carol Todd, Barbara Maier, Ula Nicewicz—how does one achieve success without some strong and cool women around to cheer you on? I wouldn't know. Derek Todd, Ethan

Kelley, Robin Robinson, James Young, Adam Williams, Craig Thompson, what upstanding men you are. Thanks for your help and inspiration. And Doug Macfarlane, while you are no longer here with us, I don't forget you. I know how proud you would have been to see this book come to life.

## FOOD, WINE, AND SPIRIT READERS
Pascaline Lepeltier, when I met you I thought, "Wow, what a badass," and then when I got to know you that thought remained the same. I love our wine and whiskey chart. Thank you. Diana Pittet and chef Rob Bleifer, thanks for your whiskey and food pairing input. Alex Valencia and Hemant Pathak, let anyone take the challenge and try making better whiskey cocktails than you two. I'm honored that you worked on this book with me.

## THE BOOK TEAM
Thank you, Lucia Watson and Gigi Campo. What a lucky person I am to be working with you at Viking Studio. You are both kind and patient, and talented at what you do. And thank you to Beth Parker, publicist extraordinaire. Gratitude to Kim Witherspoon and Charlie Olsen at Inkwell Management. Kim, you're so suave that you make things happen by sitting there and willing it, silently. At least that's what it looks like to me. And Charlie, you took a break from reading graphic novels to sell my book, then answered one million phone calls, and continued to be an awesome person at the same time. Can we drink some whiskey now?

---

THANKS TO MY LOUD, LOVING, AND VIBRANT
GREENE-GERSHOFF–HURLEY-ORR FAMILY,
AND ESPECIALLY TO MY HUSBAND, THE ONLY
MATT GERSHOFF IN THE WHOLE WORLD.

# Appendix: Whiskey for the Wine Lover

## TABLE 7: WINE VERSUS WHISKEY QUICK-VIEW CHART

I've created a wine versus whiskey quick-view chart with world-renowned sommelier Pascaline Lepeltier of Rouge Tomate in New York City to help you identify some key differences between the wine and whiskey worlds in a snapshot. It is based on the common questions I've received from wine geeks who want to change camps for a while and join us whiskey nerds.

| PRODUCTION | WHISKEY | WINE | KEEP IN MIND |
|---|---|---|---|
| Raw Material | Grain | Grapes | The most popular grains used in whiskey are barley, corn, rye, and wheat. Most of the wines you enjoy are made from the *Vitis vinifera*—a grape species. |

| PRODUCTION | WHISKEY | WINE | KEEP IN MIND |
|---|---|---|---|
| Yeast | Yes | Yes | Whiskey makers manipulate yeast to play with flavor. America and Japan are at the forefront of experimentation.<br><br>Winemakers can choose to "spontaneously ferment" with yeasts found in the environment (that is, on skins, in the winery) or, like whiskey, inoculate with very specific strains in order to obtain very specific results. |
| Terroir | Influence is debatable and most evident when comparing major producing regions like America versus Scotland (rather than within Scotland or America). | Influence is paramount and defining—even though you may find different interpretations and definitions. | Whiskey is more craftsmanship than terroir, though some element of terroir can come into play. A producer can override effects of terroir and often does.<br><br>Wine is driven by a sense of place, down to a plot of land in which the grapes grew. Geography, climate, and geology are all important factors. Winemakers don't mess with terroir the way that whiskey producers may. |

| PRODUCTION | WHISKEY | WINE | KEEP IN MIND |
|---|---|---|---|
| Distillation | Yes | No, except in fortified wines like sherry, port, and Madeira. Whiskey uses a distilled spirit in production. | The type of still shape and style will affect whiskey output and flavor.<br><br>In fortified wines, the type of still used is not important; instead, the timing of when the distilled spirit is added and the type of spirit will have an important impact on the result. |
| Fermentation | Yes | Yes. Plus wine may also go through another fermentation called the malolactic fermentation. | Both use yeast to eat sugars, which convert to alcohol. In whiskey, yeast feeds off the sugary grain liquid; in wine, yeast feeds off sugars from the grapes. In wine, a secondary malolactic fermentation can take place that changes the acid structure of the wines and may alter some aromas. It is standard for producing red wine to create a fuller mouthfeel. |
| Filtration | Yes. Chill filtration, but not always | Yes. Many kinds of filtering techniques to clarify; also called "fining" but not always. | Both whiskey and wine can go through filtering processes to take out elements such as fatty acids and other insoluble elements. It is a matter of personal taste on the part of both the producer and the consumer with how "clear" the liquid needs to be. |

| PRODUCTION | WHISKEY | WINE | KEEP IN MIND |
|---|---|---|---|
| Bottling | Year-round | Seasonally | Whiskey can be bottled when a cask is ready, at any time of year. Usually wine is bottled once a year, with exceptions: specifically, sparkling wines. |
| Water | Yes. Often added before bottling | Most of the time, no water is added before bottling, but certain warmer wine regions authorized up to 25% water addition in order to decrease the high sugar/potential alcohol content. | Whiskey bottled without added water is called "cask strength." Most whiskey companies add water to bring the ABV down. |

| KEEPING | WHISKEY | WINE | CONSIDERATIONS |
|---|---|---|---|
| Aging | In cask | In bottle | The moment a whiskey comes out of a cask, the aging process stops. Wine continues to age in the bottle and can do so for years (even with a screw cap). |
| Storage | Upright | On its side, in a temperature- and humidity-controlled room—in the dark, if possible, and away from vibration (especially if you live by the subway in NYC) | Whiskey is not as sensitive as wine, but do not expose it to extreme temperatures or light for best results. Properly stored, unopened whiskey should last many years. |

| KEEPING | WHISKEY | WINE | CONSIDERATIONS |
|---|---|---|---|
| Age Statement | Indicates minimum years aged in a cask | Indicates grape harvest year = the definition of "vintage" | Wine is all about vintage (year) except for nonvintage Champagnes and other sparkling and fortified wines. With whiskey, consistency of distillery character is key, with the exception of single barrel or single cask whiskeys that can vary in palate slightly. |
| Color | From wood properties | From grape varietal | The color of your whiskey will change because of the years it spends in the cask, type of cask, and the type of spirit the cask once contained. Some producers use caramel coloring. Grapes determine wine color, though there are some tricks the winemaker can use to modify/ intensify it. |
| ABV | Minimum 40% | Between 1.2% (Tokaji Eszencia) and 22% (vin de liqueur) | Both will get you drunk, if you drink too much. Neither will give you a better or worse hangover, despite the myths. |

| KEEPING | WHISKEY | WINE | CONSIDERATIONS |
|---|---|---|---|
| Are there special years to look for? | No. Consistency year to year is key with whiskey core-range bottles. | Yes. Different harvests yield different aromatics and tastes. | Wine bottlings celebrate certain grape harvests, which result in exceptional years and differences in a wine's personality each year. Whiskey remains relatively consistent from year to year, with the exception of single barrel whiskeys or special releases/ limited editions. These are tweaked expressions that have the same overall distillery characteristics. Whiskey makers don't look for special grain-harvest years. |
| How long after a bottle is opened can I drink it? | A long time, possibly years, if stored well | Within a day or so | Whiskey can be kept on your shelf for a very long time; oxidation happens very slowly over time. Watch the ratio of liquid to oxygen in a bottle. Wine must be enjoyed within days as its compounds oxidize rapidly. |
| Top Producing Countries | Scotland, France, Ireland, Canada, Japan | France, Italy, Spain, Germany, Austria, U.S.A., and on and on . . . | Keep in mind that new producers are popping up all over the world in both the wine and whiskey industries. |

| KEEPING | WHISKEY | WINE | CONSIDERATIONS |
|---|---|---|---|
| Big Name Producers Versus Small Producers | Often called "craft," but even large producers co-opt the term. | Often called "small growers" versus big brand houses of Negoce | Don't fall for "smaller is better" or "big is bad" for either wine- or whiskey makers. In general, larger wine- and whiskey makers will produce more consistent, ready-to-drink products; small producers can often present a wider, rougher variance in taste and styles. |

| EVALUATION | WHISKEY | WINE | CONSIDERATIONS |
|---|---|---|---|
| Sight | Attention to color and clarity: Cloudy whiskey indicates non–chill filtered whiskey. | Attention to clarity, color, presence of gas, sediments, and "legs" running down the side of a glass. | Some whiskey is colored with caramel coloring (more common in Scotch). Looking at a wine's "legs" is an essential component of wine evaluation. Some whiskeys have legs and some don't. ABV doesn't vary as much. |

| EVALUATION | WHISKEY | WINE | CONSIDERATIONS |
|---|---|---|---|
| Nose | Approach with caution and don't stick your nose too far into a glass. Whiskey always is a minimum 40% ABV. Gently inhale aromas as you bring the glass toward your nose to get the perfumes. | Start with a precise and short sniff so you don't saturate your olfactory bulb. Then follow with a few long, intense sniffings, multiple short ones, anything you like. Your nose can be deep into the glass. | The lower ABV in wine allows for a deeper and quicker comprehension of aromas. In whiskey, you must nose *through* the high ABV to get at the aromas, while taking great care not to stimulate the pain receptors. Try to start by identifying the first nose (the aromas you can pick up with no swirling of the glass), especially the lightest compounds. Then swirl in order to reveal heavier esters—what we call the second nose. |
| Palate | You can't discern the differences in whiskeys based on tongue taste only. Focus more on the nose and the interplay of nose and tongue (palate). | More elements are revealed in wine on the tongue than in whiskey, but the interplay of the nose and tongue is also important in wine. | You can chew and swish both wine and whiskey. Finish, mouthfeel, texture, bitterness, sweetness, and retronasal olfaction of aromas are all important experiences for understanding both wine and whiskey. |

## DO YOU LOVE YOUR SHERRY-INFLUENCED SCOTCH? YOU DO? THEN TRY THIS!

Pascaline and I once taught a class titled Whiskey for the Wine Lover at her esteemed restaurant. Before getting up and speaking in front of a group of colleagues in the industry and press, though, I sent her a series of whiskeys to nose and taste. Based on the aromatic compounds and mouthfeel of the whiskeys I sent, Pascaline developed complementary wine recommendations. Here is a quick chart for you based on that class. You can use this chart to find a whiskey based on your own wine preferences, or you can find a wine style based on knowing what whiskeys you like best. The chart can be used both ways. While we can't list every single brand of whiskey or wine that might work here, we hope this helps you narrow down the types of wines or whiskeys that relate to one another should you be preparing a dinner menu, reading a restaurant list, or buying spirits as gifts.

## WHISKEY FOR THE WINE LOVER CHART

| STYLE | A FEW BRAND EXAMPLES | WINE CHARACTERISTICS | RED | WHITE | SPARKLING | KEY PERSONALITY TRAITS |
|---|---|---|---|---|---|---|
| Smoked and Peated Scotch | Laphroaig<br>Caol Ila<br>Ardbeg<br>Bowmore<br>Lagavulin | Terroir = Volcanic soil, coastal region for white, northern, sedimentary (fossils) soils<br><br>Vinification = A certain amount of *Brettanomyces* (a certain type of yeast), barrel with high toast, wines with some age; for the white, some skin contact | France = Old Bordeaux and Rhône (15, 20+ years old), Loire Valley Cabernet Franc<br>Italy = Old Piemonte (15, 20+ years old), Sicilia<br>Spain = Baleares<br>U.S.A. = Old California (15, 20+ years old)<br>South America = Mission/Pais/Carmenere–based wine | France = Aged Chablis and Muscadet<br>Italy/Slovenia = Fiano from Campania, Sicilia, skin contact<br>Spain = Traditional Rioja<br>Greece = Assyrtiko<br>Portugal = Vinho Verde made with Loureiro<br>Australia = Hunter Valley Semillon<br>All = Orange wines | Aged vintage Champagne | Iodine<br>Brine<br>The sea<br>Oiliness<br>Seaweed<br>Flint |

| STYLE | A FEW BRAND EXAMPLES | WINE CHARACTERISTICS | RED | WHITE | SPARKLING | KEY PERSONALITY TRAITS |
|---|---|---|---|---|---|---|
| Sherry-Influenced Scotch | The Macallan GlenDronach The Dalmore Glenfarclas | Terroir = Limestone, clay, gravel, moderate climate<br><br>Vinification = White with malolactic fermentation, sweetness from the oak treatment (blond toast, new oak) | France = Southern Rhône Valley from a cooler vintage, Graves, and Pessac-Léognan<br>Italy = Brunello, Chianti of Tuscany<br>Spain = Traditional Rioja<br>Greece = Xinomavro | France = Chardonnay from Burgundy and Jura, Roussanne/ Marsanne from the Rhône Valley, Vin Jaune<br>Italy/Slovenia = White Friulian/ Collio/Brda<br>Austria = Smaragd from the Wachau (Grüner Veltliner)<br>USA = Old California Chardonnay | Solera-based Champagne, recently disgorged | Figs<br>Raisins<br>Chocolate<br>Toffee<br>Sulfur<br>Walnut<br>Curry<br>Apple skin |

| STYLE | A FEW BRAND EXAMPLES | WINE CHARACTERISTICS | RED | WHITE | SPARKLING | KEY PERSONALITY TRAITS |
|---|---|---|---|---|---|---|
| Nonpeated, Nonsherried Scotch, World Malts | Glenfiddich Yamazaki Glenmorangie (Nectar D'or) St. George | Terroir = Cool to moderate climate, with a large variation of soil. Vinification = Nothing extreme, for the white ripe, but on the drier side, with medium- to full-bodied grape; red | France = Pinot Noir (Burgundy, Alsace, Loire) Italy = Piemonte, Lombardy, Veneto Spain = Rioja U.S.A. = Oregon Pinot | France = Loire Valley Chenin, Dry Alsatian Riesling Germany = Grosses Gewächs Italy = White Piemonte Austria = Wachau Grüner Veltliner and Riesling South Africa = Chenin | Blend, Pinot Meunier blend, Brut | Citrus Florals Honey Grass Nuts Salt |

| STYLE | A FEW BRAND EXAMPLES | WINE CHARACTERISTICS | RED | WHITE | SPARKLING | KEY PERSONALITY TRAITS |
|---|---|---|---|---|---|---|
| Big American Rye | High West<br>Old Overholt<br>Knob Creek Rye | Terroir = Warmer region, clay, alluvial, limestone soil<br><br>Vinification = In new oak, eventually American | France = Young northern Rhône, southwest, Pomerol<br><br>Italy = Super Tuscan<br><br>Spain = Ribera del Duero, New Rioja, Priorat<br><br>U.S.A. = California Cabernet Sauvignon, Merlot or Bordeaux blend<br><br>Australia = Victoria's Syrah<br><br>South Africa = Syrah or Syrah blend from Stellenbosch, Swartland | France = Alsatian Pinot Gris, White Bordeaux<br><br>Spain = White Priorat, Rueda<br><br>Australia = Victoria/Adelaide Hills Chardonnay, McLaren Vale Sauvignon Blanc | Barrel fermented with some dosage, if possible Pinot based; Franciacorta, Cava Reserva/Gran Reserva | Orange rind<br>Pepper<br>Clove<br>Vanilla<br>Earl Grey<br>Tobacco<br>Fern |

| STYLE | A FEW BRAND EXAMPLES | WINE CHARACTERISTICS | RED | WHITE | SPARKLING | KEY PERSONALITY TRAITS |
|---|---|---|---|---|---|---|
| Big American Bourbon | Buffalo Trace Four Roses Michter's Woodford Reserve | Terroir = Warmer region Vinification = Concentration, new oak (American); ripe, rich extraction, eventually a little residual sugar | France = Southern Rhône and Languedoc Grenache/Syrah Italy = Southern Italy, Amarone, Aglianico U.S.A. = California Grenache blend, Zinfandel, Washington Australia = South Australia (Barossa, Coonawarra, McLaren Vale) Argentina = Malbec | France = Condrieu/ Viognier U.S.A. = California Chardonnay Australia = Chardonnay, Rhône blend (Roussanne/ Marsanne/ Viognier) | Barrel fermented, if possible Pinot based; Brut too dry for the dosage | Vanilla Almond Coconut Spice Molasses |

| STYLE | A FEW BRAND EXAMPLES | WINE CHARACTERISTICS | RED | WHITE | SPARKLING | KEY PERSONALITY TRAITS |
|---|---|---|---|---|---|---|
| Floral, Light, Approachable Irish Whiskey | Tullamore Dew<br>Redbreast<br>Knappogue Castle | Terroir = Moderate climate, granitic soil<br>Vinification = Low extraction for red (carbonic maceration), neutral vessel fermentation for white with some lees contact, pyrozine/thiols grapes | France = Beaujolais/Gamay<br>Italy = Valpolicella, Dolcetto<br>U.S.A. = Oregon/California Pinot Noir | France = Sancerre, Sauvignon Blanc, Jurançon Sec<br>Spain = Rias Baixas<br>Italy = Friulian Pinot Grigio<br>Germany = Mosel Riesling (Kabinett or Spätlese Trocken) | Pinot Meunier, Chardonnay based, lower dosage; Prosecco (Cremant d'Alsace, de Loire, de Bourgogne, etc.); German Sekt | Green apple<br>Floral<br>Lemon<br>Grass<br>Elderflower<br>Pear |
| Edgy, Young Craft Whiskeys | Tuthilltown<br>Kings County<br>Balcones | Terroir = Most of the time, the underdog wine regions<br>Vinification = Low intervention, no additives in the winegrowing or the winemaking but a little sulfur | The so-called natural wine, low intervention movement, active now in nearly all wine countries | The so-called natural wine, low intervention movement, active now in nearly all wine countries | Grower Champagne, low to no dosage | Grainy<br>Bold<br>Rustic<br>Full of personality |

# References and Resources

I'VE READ THESE BOOKS over the years, all of which I recommend for further whiskey study.

Barleycorn, Michael. *Moonshiner's Manual*. Hayward, California: White Mule Press, 1975.

Broom, David. *The World Atlas of Whisky*. London, UK: Octopus Publishing Group Ltd, 2010.

Cowdery, Charles K. *Bourbon, Strait: The Uncut and Unfiltered Story of American Whiskey*. Chicago: Made and Bottled in Kentucky, 2004.

De Kerginneax, Davin. *Canadian Whiskey: The Portable Expert*. Toronto, Ontario, Canada: McClelland & Stewart Ltd, 2012.

Herz, Rachel. *The Scent of Desire: Discovering Our Enigmatic Sense of Smell*. New York: HarperCollins, 2007.

Minnick, Fred. *Whiskey Women: The Untold Story of How Women Saved Bourbon, Scotch, and Irish Whiskey*. Dulles, VA: Potomac Books, 2013.

Veach, Michael R. *Kentucky Bourbon Whiskey: An American Heritage*. Lexington, KY: University of Kentucky Press, 2013.

Watman, Max. *Chasing the White Dog: An Amateur Outlaw's Adventures in Moonshine*. New York: Simon & Schuster, 2010.

## WHISKEY WEB SITES

Caskstrength.blogspot.com
Chuckcowderyblogspot.com
Connosr.com
Discus.org
Dramming.com
Drinkhacker.com
fredminnick.com
Jewmalt.com
Maltmadness.com

Maltmaniacs.net
misswhisky.com  (Yes, that's a woman behind this one!)
recenteats.blogspot.com
Scotchandicecream.com
therewillbebourbon.net
whiskyadvocateblog.com
Whiskyscienceblogspot.com

# Index